R. Gupta's®

PREPOSITIONS

&

THEIR USAGE

By

H.S. BHATIA

Ramesh Publishing House, New Delhi

Published by
O.P. Gupta *for* Ramesh Publishing House

Admin. Office
12-H, New Daryaganj Road, Opp. Officers' Mess,
New Delhi-110002 ☎ 23261567, 23275224, 23275124

E-mail: info@rameshpublishinghouse.com
Website: www.rameshpublishinghouse.com

Showroom
● Balaji Market, Nai Sarak, Delhi-6 ☎ 23253720, 23282525
● 4457, Nai Sarak, Delhi-6, ☎ 23918938

Book Code: R-787

ISBN: 978-93-5012-633-2

18th Edition : 1801

HSN Code: 49011010

CONTENTS

1. Prepositions (General) 7

2. Use of Important Prepositions 15

3. Phrase Prepositions 40

4. Participial Prepositions 44

5. Prepositions and Nouns—I 46

6. Prepositions and Nouns—II 51

7. Prepositions and Nouns—III 54

8. Prepositions Adjectives and Participles 63

9. Prepositions and Verbs 75

10. Prepositions and Adverbs 89

11. Prepositions and Conjunctions 95

12. Use of Prepositions as Other Parts of Speech 98

13. Compound Prepositions 104

14. Prepositions as Affixes 106

15. Use of Prepositions in Phrases,
Idioms & Proverbs 124

16. Words Followed by Prepositions
(Without sentence) 160

17. Use of Prepositions 211

18. Use of Prepositions (Long Sentences & Passages) .. 220

19. Use of Prepositions (Running Passages) 227

20. Choosing the Right Alternative—I 237

21. Choosing the Right Alternative—II 254

22. Test Papers—I 267

23. Test Papers—II 273

24. Test Papers–III 284

Prepositions
and
their Usage

1. PREPOSITIONS
(General)

It is rightly said that prepositions form an important adornment of the English language. If it is so, they deserve a special attention.

It will not be wrong if we assert that the maximum number of errors committed by an average writer are in the use of prepositions.

The proper use of prepositions is, indeed, such a tricky affair that many a time even the most learned ones feel baffled.

We'll have to admit that among the greatest controversies that converge on the whole lot of grammarians is in the matter of the use of prepositions.

The baffling conglomeration of prepositions is like a wild bull and must likewise be handled most carefully and valiantly like a brave matador. Let's hope that we are such a one when we work in unison with the best of intensity and methological penetration of understanding. Let the pages that follow unfold the treasuresome aspects of these gems, the prepositions that deserve to be valued as such.

Let's first of all make a tentative list of prepositions even if we do not pursue the usage of each of them with boring doggedness. The list may at places look strange to some readers, but this is as it should look till the unfolding process is brought home by stages—

1. At
2. But
3. From
4. In
5. On
6. Above
7. Beneath
8. Over
9. To
10. With
11. Within
12. Like
13. Against
14. Between
15. Among
16. Near
17. By
18. Upon
19. Under
20. Below
21. Up
22. Down
23. Out of
24. Outside
25. Inside
26. Toward
27. Towards
28. For
29. Of
30. Off
31. Through
32. Till
33. About
34. Across
35. Along
36. Midst
37. Amidst
38. Beside
39. Beyond
40. Without
41. Underneath
42. Behind
43. Before
44. After
45. Around
46. Round
47. Per
48. Since
49. Except
50. Until
51. Into
52. Than
53. Next
54. During
55. Past
56. Athwart
57. Along
58. Besides
59. Betwixt

EXERCISE-1

Underline the prepositions in the following sentences:—

1. He acted upon my advice.
2. The little girl sat in a corner.
3. There are many flower-plants in this garden.
4. He is like his father.
5. All except him began to weep.
6. None but Prem was absent.
7. It is not within my powers.
8. How much do you earn per month?
9. Do not stay inside the room.
10. You can have this pen without paying a penny.
11. We should not go there before sunrise.
12. We reached home after sunset.
13. I can say this without hesitation.
14. We saw him outside the cinema hall.
15. Wait here till sunset.
16. He will not come until five o'clock.
17. Oranges are sold by the dozen.
18. It is all into the bargain.
19. Your words are beside the mark.
20. I'm with you in this matter.
21. I am convinced of your honesty.
22. Do not beat about the bush.
23. He is much worried about the health of his old father.
24. I read in fifth class.
25. The child is sitting in the shade of the tree.

26. The sky is above us all.
27. Put the liquid on the stove.
28. Do not go near the lion.
29. Distribute these mangoes between the two brothers.
30. Distribute these alms among the five beggars.
31. She is suffering from fever.
32. I can say nothing beyond this.
33. Who is behind the tree?
34. He has been working in this office since 1998.
35. Can you please go round the corner?
36. The lion jumped upon the deer.
37. You must have a deep look through the matter.
38. The weak have to go to the wall.
39. They kept dancing till midnight.
40. His house lies by the river.
41. She is a woman of great merit.
42. Please go into the hall.
43. Do not quarrel with anybody.
44. Let us sit under the tree.
45. He starts work with the sunrise.
46. The temple lies beside the lake.
47. He gave a slap across his face.
48. Who is the most intelligent among these boys?
49. The dacoits cut off the trader's head with a sword.
50. I'll return within five minutes.

ANSWERS

1.	upon	26.	above
2.	in	27.	on
3.	in	28.	near
4.	like	29.	between
5.	except	30.	among
6.	but	31.	from
7.	within	32.	beyond
8.	per	33.	behind
9.	inside	34.	in, since
10.	without	35.	round
11.	before	36.	upon
12.	after	37.	through
13.	without	38.	to
14.	outside	39.	till
15.	till	40.	by
16.	until	41.	of
17.	by	42.	into
18.	into	43.	with
19.	beside	44.	under
20.	with, in	45.	with
21.	of	46.	beside
22.	about	47.	across
23.	about, of	48.	among
24.	in	49.	with
25.	in, of	50.	within

EXERCISE-2

Point out whether the bold words in the following sentences are prepositions or not. Write [   ] Yes or No:

1. This book is **mine**.

2. I do not **like** him.

3. She is just **like** her mother.

4. Work hard to pass **the** examination.

5. He sat **by** me for two hours.

6. Wait here **till** evening.

7. Do you agree **with** him?

8. A wave of fear ran **through** the town.

9. The farmers **till** the land.

10. Please go **to** your seat.

11. Where does the sun go **at** night?

12. Death **before** dishonour.

13. All his plans fell **through**.

14. Our examinations will begin **on** Monday.

15. I am not **at** fault.

16. One of the wheels of the car came **off**.

17. Can you go **across** the river by swimming?

18. He will be back **by** five 'o' clock.

19. You'll learn by and **by**.

20. Can anybody live **without** air?

21. He was left **behind**.

22. Thereafter, they went **in**.

23. **Since** when have you been working in this office?

24. **Since** you insist I'll go there.

25. He must have learnt much **by** you.

26. They began to quarrel **over** a trifling matter.

27. Please attend **to** me.

28. This is the matter to be thought **over.**

29. Please come **in**.

30. Move **on**, please.

ANSWERS

1. No	**2.** No	**3.** Yes	**4.** No
5. Yes	**6.** Yes	**7.** Yes	**8.** Yes
9. No	**10.** Yes	**11.** Yes	**12.** Yes
13. No	**14.** Yes	**15.** Yes	**16.** No
17. Yes	**18.** Yes	**19.** No	**20.** Yes
21. No	**22.** No	**23.** Yes	**24.** No
25. Yes	**26.** Yes	**27.** Yes	**28.** Yes
29. No	**30.** No		

❦

2. Use of Important Prepositions

1. *About*

1. Tell me something *about* aeroplanes.
2. Do you know anything *about* him?
3. Have you any money *about* you?
4. I saw a rabbit somewhere *about* here.
5. Is he very particular *about* his dress?
6. What *about* having a picnic near the canal on Sunday?
7. What is he *about* now?
8. When you are *about* this job, let me attend to mine.
9. Why are you loitering *about* the streets?
10. How *about* taking Rashid with us?
11. I am having a twitching sensation *about* my left ear.
12. It is *about* seven o'clock.
13. Go *about* your work without a moment's delay.

(**Note:** In a sentence such as No. 12 above, some grammarians regard 'about' as an adverb.)

2. *Above*

1. Character is *above* everything else in life.
2. Look ! the sun has already risen *above* the horizon.
3. Children should not be taught *above* their head.
4. In a class-room, be never *above* asking questions.
5. The weight of this man is *above* sixty Kg.
6. He is *above* sixty.

7. The cost of this pen is *above* ten rupees.
8. I value character *above* all.
9. We have the sky *above* our heads.
10. You will get good perks over and *above* your salary in this company.

3. *Across*

1. My house lies *across* the river.
2. He walked *across* the street.
3. Our lorry passed over the bridge *across* the river.
4. Draw two lines which pass *across* each other at right angles.
5. Will you please row me *across* the canal?
6. Why are you standing with your arms *across* your breast.
7. I saw a strange man standing *across* the lawn.
8. He hailed me from *across* the room.

4. *After*

1. She entered the hall *after* me.
2. Most of the people run *after* riches.
3. We reached the destination *after* sunset.
4. *After* all, he is your real brother.
5. *After* all said and done, let us bury the hatchet.

5. *Against*

1. I have nothing to say *against* you.
2. She was leaning *against* the wall.
3. Do nothing *against* the interest of the country.
4. The government should do something *against* the annual floods.

5. The result of the matric class has been much better this year *against* the last year result.
6. Three hundred votes were *against* and two hundred fifty in favour of the Bill in the Parliament.
7. Do nothing *against* your conscience.
8. He is racing *against* time.

6. *Along*

1. Please go *along* the bank of the canal to reach the temple.
2. There are shady trees all *along* the road on either side.
3. This road goes *along* the rail track for about seven kilometres.
4. Pass *along* the truck, please.
5. Move *along* here, please.

7. *Around*

1. Is anybody *around* here?
2. About a dozen men stood *around* him.
3. There was a larger crowd of people *around* the place of accident.
4. Please don't put your arm *around* my neck.
5. All *around* us we saw wild animals and plants.
6. He has been *around* the whole of Europe.

8. *At*

1. I get up *at* five o'clock in the morning.
2. I am surprised *at* your strange behaviour.
3. The train arrives *at* the station *at* 11.00 a.m.
4. They could not arrive *at* any decision.
5. She is sitting *at* the study table

6. I suddenly woke up *at* night when I heard a noise in the street.

7. She lives *at* Daudpur, a small village in Distict Breilly.

8. Last night, I dined *at* my uncle's.

9. I am *at* your disposal.

10. Look *at* the blackboard.

11. He rushed *at* the enemy.

12. Do not laugh *at* the poor.

13. Those who live in glass houses should not throw stones *at* others.

14. A drowning man catches *at* a straw.

15. It can rain *at* any moment.

16. Please do not talk, the child is *at* work.

17. This child is mostly *at* play.

18. The two countries are *at* war.

19. What are you driving *at*?

20. The car is running *at* full speed.

21. The tourists were marvelled *at* the beauty of the Taj.

22. The child was delighted *at* having drawn the map of India for the first time.

23. You can do this job *at* leisure.

24. He had to sell his goods *at* a heavy loss.

25. He is good *at* mathematics.

26. He explained the whole matter *at* great length.

27. I finished this novel *at* one sitting.

28. You will have to guess *at* the moral of this story.

29. Always keep undesirable elements *at* arm's length.

30. Do not stare *at* the child.

31. What I told him went in *at* one ear and out *at* the other.

32. You can have a better look of things *at* a distance.

33. *At* no time did he indicate his willingness to help me.

34. There is a light *at* the end of the tunnel.

35. The two brothers are *at* daggers drawn with each other.

36. I get up *at* dawn.

37. He is *at* his best now.

38. He fell in love with her *at* first sight.

10. *Athwart*

1. The beam/shaft of light could be seen *athwart* floor.

11. *Before*

1. He carried all *before* him.

2. What day was it the day *before* yesterday?

3. Was this war fought *before* or after Christ?

4. I had never visited the Taj *before* then.

5. K comes *before* L.

6. Where did you work *before* joining this company?

7. *Before* long he became my friend.

8. The accused was brought *before* the judge.

9. We reached home *before* sunset.

10. Can you speak *before* a large audience?

11. Death *before* dishonour.

12. I get up *before* five o'clock.

13. Who is standing *before* the door?

(**Note:** Some grammarians regard 'before' as in sentence No.12 as an adverb.)

12. *Behind*

1. The train is *behind* schedule.

2. He stood *behind* the wall.

3. The moon was *behind* the clouds.
4. Who is *behind* this idea?
5. My house lies *behind* the hill.
6. He pulled the wires from *behind* the scenes.
7. His uncle has left a vast fortune *behind* him.
8. You are *behind* other students in the class.
9. It is difficult for one to catch up who is left *behind* times.
10. Pakistan is far *behind* India in the matter of development.
11. The cat ran *behind* the rat.
12. There is a ray of light *behind* every cloud.

13. *Below*

1. He is *below* fifty.
2. It is *below* your dignity to wear this ragged coat.
3. Her skirt reaches *below* the knees.
4. Yesterday, the temperature was *below* the freezing point.
5. Please do not write anything *below* this line.
6. While flying we have sky above and earth *below* us.
7. An accountant is *below* the manager in a bank.
8. The sun sets *below* the horizon.

14. *Beneath*

1. It is *beneath* him to indulge in idle talk.
2. All your complaints are *beneath* contempt.
3. These trivial remarks are *beneath* observation/notice.
4. We took rest *beneath* the shade of the tree.

(**Note:** The use of "beneath" in a sentence such as No. 4 above is now a days somewhat outdated.)

15. *Beside*

1. Please sit *beside* me.
2. My house is situated *beside* the Church.
3. She looks quite a pigmy *beside* you.
4. Your words are *beside* the point at issue.
5. On hearing this news, I was *beside* myself with joy.
6. No leader can be put/set *beside* Gandhiji in the observance of truth/non-violence.

16. *Besides*

1. There is none *besides* me to decide this matter.
2. This shirt of yours is too gaudy; *besides*, it looks too loose on you.
3. Three other gentlemen have sought membership of the club, *besides* you.
4. I can't accompany you to the theatre as I'am feeling unwell; *besides*, I'm expecting some guests.
5. *Besides* lending me a helping hand in the work, he helped me with money.

17. *Between*

1. *Between* two stools you fall to the ground.
2. Divide this apple *between* two boys.
3. It is *between* you and me.
4. What lies *between* the sky and the earth?
5. There is only a minor difference *between* life and death.
6. Nepal is situated *between* India and China.
7. The rank of a major is *between* a captain and a colonel.
8. He must be *between* sixty and seventy.

9. Do not take water *between* the meals.
10. Take something light *between* breakfast and lunch.
11. Where were you *between* five and six o'clock?

18. *Betwixt*

A Chimpanzee is *betwixt* man and animal.

(**Note:** (i) It means between two things or beings.

(ii) "Betwixt" is now almost archaic and is used only for literary purposes.

19. *Beyond*

1. What is there *beyond* space?
2. It is *beyond* my powers to grant you leave.
3. My house lies *beyond* that hill.
4. Her pain is *beyond* endurance.
5. Your behaviour is *beyond* all norms of civility.
6. He is a genius, *beyond* doubt.
7. I can say nothing *beyond* this in this matter.

20. *But*

1. There was none *but* him left on the playground.
2. Nothing *but* one folly after the other can be expected of him.
3. No one *but* you are right.
4. All left the place *but* Suresh.
5. Who *but* she could be expected to do this task?
6. The last *but* one boy in the row is my friend.
7. *But* for his help I would have been ruined.
8. He is an honest man *but* that he does not show it off.
9. I can't help you not *but* that what I sympathise with you.

10. Delhi is a city of problems *but* then it is also the capital of India.

21. *By*

1. Please sit *by* me.
2. I caught him *by* the collar/neck.
3. *By* whom has the cup been broken?
4. She swore *by* God/heaven that she hadn't committed the crime.
5. I get up *by* sunrise.
6. How did you get *by* this watch?
7. I'll stand *by* you.
8. Can you lift this box *by* yourself?
9. Always keep a glass of water *by* you on the table while doing office work.
10. Don't be/feel disturbed *by* trifling/minor happenings/things.
11. We went *by* the fields to reach your house.
12. He will be here *by* five o'clock.
13. The cloth is sold *by* the metre.
14. He works *by* the day and studies *by* the night.
15. The child was overrun *by* a lorry.
16. If you go *by* the post-office, please post this letter.
17. Put/lay *by* something for the rainy day.
18. He did his work *by* fits and starts.
19. I went there *by* train.
20. He was attacked *by* the robbers.
21. Our homes are lighted *by* electricity.

22. *Down*

1. He climbed *down* the tree.

  2. When will the *down* train arrive?

  3. The tears ran *down* his face as he heard this story.

  4. Who is walking *down* the street at this hour of night?

  5. It has been proved *down* the ages/centuries that only strong nation survive.

  6. Can you row *down* the stream?

  7. Her skirt hung *down* her knees.

  8. As you go further *down* the canal, you will find a ruined temple there.

  9. It is very thrilling to run *down* a hill on a bike/bicycle.

23. *For*

  1. He has been suffering from fever *for* five days.

  2. You are responsible *for* this mistake

  3. He has been imprisoned *for* life.

  4. Rotten grain is not fit *for* human consumption.

  5. He was arrested *for* having picked a quarrel with a cop/policeman.

  6. I'm ready to do anything *for* you/*for* your sake.

  7. Many people lose their heads *for* the sake of money.

  8. He was sacked *for* negligence.

  9. The sailors have set sail *for* West Indies.

10. This train is bound *for* Delhi.

11. I'll study *for* two hours.

12. He has set out *for* home.

13. He is destined *for* being a great man.

14. Here's a news *for* you.

15. All arrangements *for* the function have been completed.

16. He is preparing *for* the examination.

17. They are canvassing *for* votes.

18. Please get ready *for* the match.

19. Let's go (out) *for* a walk.

20. I read books *for* pleasure.

21. I said this only *for* fun.

24. *From*

1. He prevented me *from* going there.

2. Look at this problem *from* different angles.

3. His house is situated far *from* here.

4. She is suffering *from* fever.

5. We want freedom *from* hunger and fear.

6. He was dressed in white *from* top to bottom.

7. He works *from* morning till evening

8. The bees go *from* flower to flower to gather honey.

9. This picture is worth-seeing *from* beginning to end.

10. He has risen *from* rags to riches.

11. Today I have received a loving letter *from* my mother.

12. This is a quotation *from* Pope.

13. Steel is made *from* iron.

14. You can get some consolation *from* this petty gain in business.

15. He died *from* exhaustion.

16. This pen differs *from* that.

17. You can't judge a man *from* his dress.

18. Many students stayed awayed *from* classes yesterday.

19. On his journey through the forests, he drank *from* brooks and streams.

20. He was released *from* prison yesterday.

21. He had to do this *from* necessity.

22. She hails *from* Hong Kong.

25. *In*

1. They are sitting *in* the room
2. It is very hot *in* plains during summer.
3. This book is two *in* one.
4. The stars are visible at night *in* fine weather.
5. Did you participate *in* the match?
6. I will come back *in* five minutes.
7. What is there *in* this box?
8. He has failed *in* science.
9. My brother lives *in* Chennai.
10. A function was held *in* memory of the late leader.
11. She was born *in* India.
12. Lions are found *in* some forests of Asia.
13. She lives *in* West Bengal.
14. He keeps lying *in* bed till seven o'clock.
15. He is *in* jail for having committed a murder.
16. There is much noise *in* the market.
17. Were you present *in* the party?
18. What was decided *in* the meeting?
19. He has gone for a holiday *in* Switzerland.
20. She is sitting *in* an arm chair.
21. My brother has been working *in* this factory for two years.
22. Flowers bloom *in* spring.
23. He died *in* the prime of his life.
24. She died *in* harness.
25. Do not move about bare-headed *in* the sun.
26. There are many flower-beds *in* this garden.
27. Fishes swim *in* the ocean.
28. Please sit down *in* a ring.

29. Are you *in* a hurry?

30. Prices of goods rise *in* time of war.

31. Take care not to commit such an error *in* future.

32. *In* the past there used to be a crockery shop here.

33. *In* which class do you read?

34. *In* which class have you passed the examination?

35. The new secretary is very much *in* action.

36. Please explain the whole matter *in* the light of the new facts.

37. Don't sit *in* the dark.

38. Don't read *in* the light of the moon.

39. A small stool is lying *in* the corner of the room.

40. Stars shine *in* the sky.

41. A soft breeze blows *in* the morning.

42. I had a ride *in* the new car.

43. The poor fishes have frozen *in* the lake.

44. The Gita is read *in* every house of the Hindus.

45. Please cut this apple *in* two.

46. The young lovers fell *in* love at first sight.

47. They never fail who fail *in* a noble cause.

48. I'll follow *in* the footsteps of my father.

49. They are sailing *in* the same boat.

50. Do not put all your eggs *in* one basket.

51. I am *in* the dark about this matter.

52. The poor beggar woman is *in* rags.

53. This car is *in* good condition.

54. White-washing is going on *in* this house.

55. Do not take any decision *in* my absence.

56. He called me names *in* the presence of Rajneesh.

57. What have you to say *in* the end?

58. She is dressed *in* white.

59. He is still *in* his teens.

60. Often one has to face several physical problems *in* old age.

61. She was born *in* 1980.

62. Many people died of starvation *in* the reign of Shah Jehan.

63. He is *in* a mood of fun.

64. I do not find anything of a wise man *in* him.

65. Not one *in* ten of people can claim to be truthful these days.

66. It is a blessing *in* disguise.

67. On hearing this, people came out *in* the streets.

68. Hyenas often hunt *in* packs.

69. You should not say such words *in* public.

70. Do not wash your dirty linen *in* public.

71. He told me this fact *in* secret.

72. The two fellows are hand *in* glove with each other.

73. I saw him *in* good health.

74. Put these books *in* proper order.

75. She seems to be *in* despair.

76. Let us have a walk *in* the moon-light.

77. The prisoner was held *in* irons/fetters.

78. How many workers are there *in* all *in* this factory?

79. Please write *in* ink.

80. Let us have the agreement *in* black and white.

81. I would like to publish this book *in* two colours.

82. He has enlisted *in* the army.

83. There is much merit *in* his words.
84. He was killed *in* action.
85. No action is wrong *in* itself except when it is done with bad intentions.
86. Please keep *in* touch with him.
87. He is superior to me *in* intellect though not *in* physical strength.
88. *In* so far as a common man is concerned, he has to work hard all his life.
89. She adopted Indian citizenship *in* 1990.
90. He is lacking *in* wit.
91. She paints *in* oil.
92. Will you like to pay by cheque or *in* cash?
93. The Taj is a dream *in* marble.
94. His statue was cast *in* bronze.
95. Do not talk *in* a loud voice.
96. They were talking *in* whispers.
97. I spend my leisure time *in* gardening.
98. A lure for money is bad *in* that it makes enemies of real brothers.
99. He is blind *in* one eye.
100. This piece of cloth is five metres *in* length.

26. *Inside*

1. What is there *inside* this box?
2. Don't let anybody come *inside* the room.
3. Please don't stand *inside* the door.

27. *Into*

1. Come *into* the room, please.
2. Do not throw this piece of meat *into* the fire.
3. Why are you trying to get *into* trouble through your foolish activities?
4. She burst *into* tears at his rude remarks.
5. Soon drizzling changed *into* a heavy down pour.
6. The goat fell *into* the well.
7. The frog jumped *into* the pond.
8. She was frightened *into* submission.
9. Let this old car be brought *into* use.
10. Do you know what is two *into* two?

28. *Like*

1. You should not behave *like* your younger brother.
2. This cap fits you *like* a glove.
3. She behaves *like* a queen.
4. You must behave *like* good boys.

29. *Of*

1. This matter is *of* great importance.
2. It is a point *of* honour for me.
3. He was convicted *of* murder.
4. He was accused *of* having stolen the purse.
5. This matter is *of* no mean consequence/importance.
6. He is a man *of* principle/few words.
7. *Of* what use is all your eloquence?
8. Our class consists *of* fifty students.
9. I am *of* the opinion that he is a rogue.
10. Birds *of* a feather flock together.
11. India has got a good reserve for foreign exchange.

12. It could'nt have happened *of* itself.

13. He did not go there for fear *of* death.

14. There is much loss *of* power during transmission.

15. I saw a bird *of* many colours.

16. She is a woman *of* great ability.

17. What was the cause *of* his death?

18. Complete this work by the 10th *of* July.

19. She is hard *of* hearing.

20. He is blind *of* one eye.

21. The five *of* us can't be accommodated in this small car.

22. It is kind *of* you to help us in this hour *of* need.

30. *Off*

1. The child fell *off* the roof of the house.

2. She was taken *off* her guard.

3. Mauritius is an island *off* the West of India.

4. Your remarks are *off* the point at issue.

5. This statement is *off*-the-record.

(**Note :** 'Off-the-record' is normally treated as one word and is as such regarded as an adjective instead of a preposition 'off' would be a preposition if it were not considered to form a compound word with 'the' and 'record'.)

6. I'm free from duty/work/employment at the moment.

7. A button has come off his shirt.

31. *On*

1. The book is lying on the table.

2. He was born *on* 5th May in 1980.

3. *On* this day last year we were at Dehradun.

4. He said these words *on* oath.

5. These words are written on the fifth page of this book.
6. *On* what terms are you ready to undertake this job?
7. I did this *on* my own.
8. *On* no account I'll allow this to be done.
9. He was allowed to attend the meeting *on* the condition that he would not be having a voting right.
10. His appointment was made *on* the terms mentioned in the appointment letter.
11. I visited my aunt's *on* Saturday last.
12. The cow lives *on* grass.
13. Our forces made a direct attack *on* the enemy.
14. Can you speak *on* this topic?
15. He disclosed these facts *on* the condition of anonymity.
16. I'm *on* good terms with him.
17. They are not *on* speaking terms with each other.
18. He is *on* fast today.
19. The enemy is *on* the run.
20. I congratulated him *on* his success in the examination.
21. *On* both sides of the canal there were trees.
22. He has retired *on* pension.
23. The patient is *on* glucose.
24. He is *on* the wrong side of eighty.
25. The train is arriving *on* time.
26. He got a lot of wealth *on* the death of his father.
27. Please hang these clothes *on* the wire.
28. He insists *on* visiting to Taj again.
29. He sat *on* my right (side).
30. I gave him a box (blow) *on* the ear.
31. I go to school *on* foot.

32. I have no money *on* me.

33. You can get more pudding *on* demand.

34. He gave me the whole information *on* my asking.

35. He was able to grab a large estate *on* the sly.

32. *Out of*

1. He proved (is) a devil *out of* machine.

2. You have to attempt any four *out of* five questions.

3. I am *out of* pocket these days.

4. She spoke these words *out of* anger/despair.

5. The whole matter has got *out of* my mind.

6. Can fish live *out of* water?

7. Please get *out of* my way.

8. A frog jumped *out of* the lake.

9. *Out of* sight, *out of* mind.

10. He ran fast and got *out of* breath.

11. This kind of pants is now *out of* fashion.

12. The machine has gone *out of* order.

13. The patient is now *out of* danger.

14. He is *out of* job these days.

15. Nothing comes *out of* nothing.

33. *Outside*

1. Who is there *outside* the door?

2. The train stopped *outside* the railway station.

3. Do you study any books *outside* those prescribed in syllabus?

4. There was much noise *outside* the house.

5. We can't assert ourselves *outside* the knowledge proved by science.

34. *Over*

1. He was thinking *over* his past.
2. The sun shines *over* the earth.
3. Please spread a cloth *over* the table.
4. Ashoka reigned *over* a vast empire.
5. His fame spread all *over* the world.
6. The cat jumped *over* the wall.
7. He is *over* ninety.
8. You will get perks *over* and above your salary.
9. We will talk about this matter *over* a cup of tea.
10. I cannot accept anybody *over* me in this office.
11. A mat of green grass spread all *over* the field/hill.

35. *Past*

1. It is five *past* ten now.
2. He is *past* all sense of shame.
3. My house lies *past* this hill.
4. Your conduct is *past* the norms of civility.

36. *Round*

1. There is a general merchant's shop *round* the corner.
2. The earth moves *round* the sun.
3. They sat *round* the fire.
4. I'm ready to spend *round* ten thousand rupees for the renovation of my house.
5. We went *round* all the beauty spots while at Shimla.
6. Please show me *round* this historical building.
7. She is wearing a scarf *round* her neck.

37. *Since*

1. He has been absent from office *since* Monday last.

2. It has been raining *since* morning.

3. He has never visited this place *since* his marriage.

4. I have not forgotten him *since* my last meeting with him in 2002.

38. *Than*

1. Nobody other *than* a postgraduate can apply for this post.

2. I'll not accept less *than* two thousand rupees for this job.

3. She is taller *than* me.

Note: Some grammarians treat 'than' in a sentence like No.3 above as a conjuction.

39. *Till*

1. We'll wait for him *till* five o'clock.

2. We'll stay here *till* you ask us to.

3. Goodbye *till* we meet next.

4. He works from morning *till* late at night.

5. Do not put off *till* tomorrow what you can do today.

40. *To*

1. Always keep *to* the left.

2. Hard work is the key *to* success.

3. We should remain loyal *to* the country.

4. This road leads *to* Bangalore.

5. We'll fight *to* the last man.

6. Who is coming *to* dinner tonight?

7. None of his friends came *to* enquire after his health.

8. *To* all appearances, he is a knave.
9. The ball fell *to* the ground.
10. Turn *to* the left from here.
11. I haven't given thought *to* it.
12. Did you stay *to* the end of the function?
13. Have you come *to* any conclusion?
14. It is a quarter *to* nine.
15. I prefer coffee *to* tea.
16. Sri Lanka is the *to* south of India.
17. Everybody was moved *to* tears on hearing his story.
18. My pen is superior *to* that.
19. You should give more attention *to* your dress/spellings.
20. The quarrel is coming *to* a head.
21. He is slow *to* excitement.
22. He tried his best *to* achieve his goal, but all *to* no purposes.
23. *To* whom did you give my pen?
24. This painting/picture/story/poem is true *to* life.
25. We should be true *to* our friends.
26. He objected *to* my remarks.

41. *Through*

1. It kept raining *through* the day.
2. Gas is leaking *through* the hole in the pipe.
3. He has got *through* the examination.
4. She had to pass *through* a tough test.
5. All *through* his life he had to work very hard.
6. I'll get this job done *through* you.

7. He joined the company *through* the backdoor/some influence.
8. He is looking *through* the microscope.
9. I looked into the room *through* the hole in the door.
10. The Yamuna flows *through* Delhi.
11. I don't think the patient will live *through* the night.
12. I heard about this matter *through* the newspaper.

42. *Toward/s*

1. We were going *toward/s* the hill.
2. My house faces *toward/s* the west.
3. What is your attitude *toward/s* his behaviour in/at the function?
4. It often grows cold *towards* the evening.
5. Prices started rising *towards* the beginning of the new year.

43. *Under*

1. He is *under* fifty.
2. We sat *under* the tree.
3. I was *under* the impression that he is a good man.
4. I'm *under* no compulsion to do this task.
5. You have laid me *under* a debt of gratitude by doing me this good turn.
6. The road is *under* repair.
7. You are *under* arrest.
8. The cat is sitting *under* the table.
9. Nobody can stay *under* water for more than a few minutes.
10. Were you flying *under* or above the clouds?

44. *Until*

1. We will wait here *until* he comes.
2. I knew nothing about him *until* he himself told me about it.
3. You should not leave this place *until* you are asked to.

45. *Up*

1. I climbed *up* the tree.
2. We sailed *up* the river.
3. We walked *up* the garden for half an hour.

46. *Upon*

1. Once *upon* a time there lived a hermit in a forest.
2. The cat jumped *upon* the table.
3. *Upon* my word, I can say all this.

(**Note** : 'on' is preferred to 'upon' in most other sentences.)

47. *With*

1. I agree *with* you.
2. I'm *with* you in this matter.
3. I can solve this problem *with* your help.
4. I'm not satisfied *with* his work.
5. All is well *with* God's grace.
6. That woman is *with* child.
7. Who is this child *with* curly hair?
8. The mountain peak is covered *with* snow.
9. I like to write *with* a pen instead of a pencil.
10. We see *with* our eyes.
11. The leaders are making speeches *with* an eye on the ensuing election.
12. Have you got any/some money *with* you?

13. I sympathise *with* you in this matter/hour of crisis.
14. Will this red go well *with* yellow?
15. He is shivering *with* cold.
16. She was trembling *with* fear.
17. Fill this bucket *with* water.
18. Who can put up (bear) *with* such insult?
19. A miser can part from a friend but not *with* money.
20. He that is not *with* me is my enemy (is against me).
21. *With* all her faults, we should love India.
22. *With* the best of his efforts, he failed to make his mark.

48. *Within*

1. It is not *within* my powers to grant you leave.
2. I'll come back *within* a week.
3. The new prosperity is not *within* the reach of the common people.
4. You must live *within* your income.
5. In rural areas women still have to remain *within* the four walls of the house.
6. Do you sleep at night *within* or without doors?

49. *Without*

1. You will have to do *without* him.
2. You can achieve nothing *without* good health.
3. Who is standing *without* the gate?
4. *Without* doubt, he is a great man.
5. We will do nothing *without* your consent.
6. Nobody can buy things *without* money.
7. We should not travel *without* a ticket.
8. It goes *without* saying that honesty pays in the long run.

3. PHRASE PREPOSITIONS

The following are some of the commonly used Phrase prepositions:—

1. Inspite of
2. Instead of
3. In lieu of
4. At the cost of
5. In favour of
6. In enmity with.
7. Because of
8. For the sake of
9. In regard to
10. In respect of
11. In reference to
12. With reference to
13. In case of
14. According to
15. In accordance with
16. With regard to
17. owing to
18. In view of
19. with an eye on
20. In order to
21. In front of
22. By means of
23. By dint of
24. By virtue of
25. In addition to
26. In respect of
27. On account of
28. In place of
29. In course of
30. In due course of
31. In conformity with
32. In compliance with
33. In the event of
34. With an eye to
35. With the connivance of
36. In consequence of
37. In comparison to
38. By way of
39. On behalf of
40. By reason of
41. Along with
42. Agreeably to
43. Conformally to
44. In consonance with

45.	In consultation with	**52.**	In pursuance of
46.	In response to	**53.**	For want of
47.	In continuation of	**54.**	In acknowledgement of
48.	In suppression of	**55.**	In quest of
49.	For the benefit of	**56.**	In view of
50.	For the reason of	**57.**	In front of
51.	In a moment of	**58.**	In keeping with

EXERCISE

Fill in the blanks with phrase prepositions in the following sentences.

1. What will you do _______ your failing in the examination?
2. He is quite _______ English.
3. He went to Delhi _______ going to Chennai.
4. What have you to say _______ your statement?
5. The Buddha set out _______ truth.
6. He passed the examination _______ hard work.
7. There is a mango tree _______ my house.
8. I have told you everything _______ this matter.
9. Everything will be done _______ your wishes.
10. His plans failed _______ funds.
11. Your written statement is _______ your spoken words.
12. We could not leave the house _______ inclement weather.
13. He could not attend the meeting _______ ill health.
14. _______ the hard work put in by him, he was given an extra increment in his salary.
15. The bill was passed in the house _______ opposition.

16. He failed __________ hard work.

17. He has not got the reward __________ the hard work put in by him.

18. He did not lose heart __________ danger.

19. The old man is __________ death.

20. __________ your advertisement in the Hindustan Times, I'm applying for the position of manager.

21. He entered the town __________ a gypsy.

22. He worked very hard __________ pass the examination.

23. __________ what I have already told you I want to say something more about the matter.

24. I have made this request to you only __________ Satish.

25. What was the political condition of India __________ Alexander's invasion?

26. The meeting has been arranged __________ your wishes.

27. __________ the tsunami thousands of families were ruined.

28. I have bought this piece of land __________ building a house on it.

29. Floods often occur in this region __________ deforestation.

30. Columbus's sailors began to dance __________ land.

31. Your helping him with money is __________ your generous nature.

32. Do you want to say anything more __________ what you have already said?

33. You will learn about the life here __________ time.

34. The clerks often take bribe __________ higher officials.

35. Please do this job __________ me.

36. Many new schemes have been started __________ lower classes of society.

37. I'm writing this letter to you _________ your communication/missive.

38. Please draw this cheque _________ Allahabad Bank.

39. I am ready to undergo any sufferings _________ my country.

40. He has decided to discontinue his studies _________ his failure in the BA Examination.

ANSWERS

1. in the event of	**21.** in the guise of
2. at home in	**22.** in order to
3. instead of	**23.** in pursuance of
4. in defence of	**24.** on behalf of
5. in quest of	**25.** on the eve of
6. by dint of	**26.** in deference to
7. in front of	**27.** in consequence of
8. in connection with	**28.** for the purpose of
9. according to/in accordance with	**29.** on account of
10. for want of	**30.** in sight of
11. at variance with	**31.** in keeping with
12. because of	**32.** in addition to
13. owing to/because of	**33.** in due course of
14. in consideration of	**34.** with the connivance of
15. in the teeth of	**35.** in consultation with
16. in spite of	**36.** for the benefit of
17. in proportion to	**37.** in acknowledgement of
18. in the face of	**38.** in favour of
19. on the brink of	**39.** for the sake of
20. with reference to	**40.** in case of

ॐ ॐ

4. PARTICIPIAL PREPOSITIONS

1. Considering
2. Regarding
3. Concerning
4. Barring
5. Notwithstanding
6. Accepting
7. Agreeing
8. Touching
9. Disregarding
10. Ignoring
11. Expressing
12. Demanding
13. Answering
14. Leading
15. Presenting
16. Praising
17. Realizing
18. Allowing
19. Forgetting
20. During

EXERCISE

Fill in the blanks in the following sentences using participial prepositions:

1. Jawaharlal Nehru wrote "Glimpses of World History" _________ his imprisonment.

2. _________ your absence from office yesterday, the officer is very angry.

3. _________ an increase in wages, the workers went on strike.

4. _________ the award to the freedom fighter, the president praised him highly.

5. _________ his own illness, the old man raised his head to bless the child.

6. _______ all the campaign against dowry system, it is still prevalent in society.

7. _________ any untoward happening, they are likely to reach this place at 6.00 p.m.

8. _________ his views on the menace of corruption, the lawyer said that strict implementation of laws was imperative.

9. _______ this matter, you must meet the manager.

10. __________ his mistake, the man apologized to me.

11. _________ the benefit of the doubt, the judge ordered that the accused should be released.

12. _________ to my proposal, the committee passed the desired resolution.

ANSWERS

1. during   **2.** regarding   **3.** Demanding

4. Presenting   **5.** Forgetting   **6.** Notwithstanding

7. Barring   **8.** Expressing   **9.** Concerning

10. Realizing   **11.** Allowing/Giving   **12.** Agreeing

❧❧

5. PREPOSITIONS AND NOUNS—I

Study the following examples where different prepositions precede or follow different nouns:

1. I am in agreement **with** you in this matter.
2. He has sent a reply in response **to** my letter.
3. You will know the real matter after perusal **of** this letter.
4. It was a moment **of** great suspense/importance.
5. This is an appendix **to** the main work.

EXERCISE

Fill in the blanks in the following sentences:

1. He has no aptitude _______ such kind of work.
2. We should have no prejudice _______ tribals.
3. I have no liking _____ fast food.
4. I have no confidence _______ him.
5. A mother's affection _______ her children is natural.
6. His infatuation _______ the gypsy girl is simply baffling.
7. Aurangzeb was a descendant _______ Akbar.
8. Can you draw any conclusion _______ a study _________ the whole matter.
9. She has no desire _________ riches.
10. Desire _______ fame is the last infirmity _________ a noble mind.
11. There is a clear contrast __________ the two situations.

12. ________ two stools you fall to the ground.

13. Your total distrust _______ your subordinates is not proper.

14. All his plans failed for want _______ funds.

15. We should show due respect ________ all.

16. He has no patience _______boastful people.

17. She took exception _______ your remarks.

18. What is your main objection ______ this project?

19. Preparations _______ the function are going on.

20. Reliance _______just one source of information is not desirable.

21. As a result _______ his tiff with the boss, he was dismissed.

22. I have great respect ______ my parents.

23. The seizure ______ contraband is allowed by international law.

24. I do not quite understand the reason _____ your dislike _____ him.

25. A child's fondness _____ toys is known to all.

26. Your complete absorption _____ humanitarian work is acknowledged by all.

27. We won't allow you the abuse ______ power.

28. Your absence _______ the party was noticed by all.

29. Repentance can lead to one's absolution _____ sin.

30. Your total abstinence in _______ meat is known to all.

31. As the corrupt leader entered the hall, he was greated with a stream _____ abuse from all sides.

32. After the death of her mother, she seems to have fallen in the abyss _____ despair.

33. There was an abundance _____ dainty dishes at the party.

34. Your remarks express a height _____ absurdity.

35. I have no access _____ the PM.

36. After his accession _____ the throne, Jehangir became wiser.

37. The progressive leader won acclamation _____ the people.

38. It is a clear violation _____ the law.

39. This is an achievement _____ no mean value.

40. On the mountain peak I saw a big accumulation _____ snow.

41. I have no acquaintance _____ such type of machines.

42. Have you got the acquaintance _____ Mr Jack?

43. It was during the eighties that he attained the acme _____ his popularity.

44. She is an asset _____ our company.

45. He spends most of his time to the acquisition _____ scientific knowledge.

46. He came out of his house in quest _____ truth.

47. His quest _____ truth goaded him to visit several countries.

48. This act _____ dishonesty committed by him deserves to be condemned.

49. Can you explain the recent advance _________ prices?

50. Did he make advances _______ you?

51. He took full advantage ______ the situation.

52. Will you please tell me something ______ his adventures _______ Central Africa?

53. Have you inserted an advertisement ______ the newspaper?

54. It is just a matter _______ a few rupees.

55. Character lies _______ truth and honesty.

56. Can you throw some light on the present state ___ affairs?

57. He has a great influence ______ the boss.

58. There is a great affinity ________ animals of the same species.

59. The affinity ______ iron ____ magnet is known to all.

60. The north pole has a great attraction _______ the south pole.

61. We should try to understand the real value _______ time.

62. What are the uses ______ forests ?

63. Please explain to me the importance _______ sports.

64. Only a few books stand the test _______ time.

65. The words ______ brackets express the accusative case _____ pronouns.

ANSWERS

1. for   **2.** against   **3.** for   **4.** in   **5.** for

6. for   **7.** of   **8.** from, of   **9.** for   **10.** for, of

11. between 12. between 13. of 14. of 15. to

16. with 17. to 18. to 19. for 20. on

21. of 22. for 23. of 24. for, of 25. for

26. in 27. of 28. from 29. from 30. from

31. of 32. of 33. of 34. of 35. to

36. to 37. of 38. of 39. of 40. of

41. with 42. of 43. of 44. to 45. of

46. of 47. for 48. of 49. in 50. to

51. of 52. about, in 53. in 54. of 55. in

56. of 57. over 58. between 59. of, for 60. for

61. of 62. of 63. of 64. of 65. in, of

❧❧

6. PREPOSITIONS AND NOUNS—II

Study the following examples of the use of prepositions before or after nouns:

1. How did she behave *at/in* the party?

2. Everything lay at sixes and sevens *in* the room.

3. There is a church *near* my house.

4. His house is *next* the temple.

5. It is a matter *of* pride for us all.

EXERCISE

Fill in the blanks with appropriate prepositions:

1. Your mind seems to be _______ confusion.

2. There is a temple ______ the vicinity ______ my house.

3. She felt upset _______ the sad news.

4. I was ________ the impression that he was a rogue.

5. People commit many crimes _________ the influence of alcohol.

6. What should be done ______ such circumstances?

7. He was released _______ the condition that he would not commit any crime again.

8. Are you _______ a hurry?

9. Life _______ peace ______ mind is useless.

10. Books are a storehouse ______ knowledge.

11. Good teachers do not teach ______ the head ______ students.

12. The result has been ______ my expectations.

13. Proper precautions __________ fire must be taken.

14. His house lies ______ my house.

15. The poor blind man hit his head _____ the post.

16. Were you rowing ______ or ________ the current?

17. Throwing garbage _____ the streets is a crime ________ many countries.

18. Honesty pays ______ the long run.

19. You must put by some money ______ a rainy day.

20. We were racing _______ time.

21. Much can be said _____ both sides.

22. I had to do this _______ my will.

23. The poor fellow is hoping ______ hope.

24. He stood up ________ a wall ______ all odds.

25. She is taller ______ me

26. Such an action is ______ law.

27. Many diseases are caused ______ the agency ______ water.

28. He got his novel published _____ an agent.

29. He conveyed this message _____ me _____ the word ______ mouth.

30. How many marks did you get _____ the aggregate?

31. Let us go there ____ strength.

32. He has been put _____ the bars.

33. We went there ____ a body.

34. Do not give airs _____ your shallow knowledge ______ this respect.

35. The goat fell ________ the well.

36. ________ working hard, he could not pass the examination.

37. ________ going to Mumbai, he has gone ________ Kolkata.

38. You must be careful ________ answering the questions.

39. Life ________ a big city is often full ______ stress and strain.

40. The words ________ italics are nouns.

ANSWERS

1. in	**2.** in, of	**3.** at
4. under	**5.** under	**6.** in
7. on	**8.** in	**9.** without, of
10. of	**11.** above, of	**12.** below
13. against	**14.** in front of	**15.** against
16. with, against	**17.** in, in	**18.** in
19. against/for	**20.** against	**21.** on
22. against	**23.** against	**24.** like, against
25. than	**26.** against	**27.** through, of
28. through	**29.** to, through, of	**30.** in
31. in	**32.** behind	**33.** in
34. to, in	**35.** into	**36.** In spite of
37. Instead of, to	**38.** in	**39.** in, of
40. in		

ॐ

7. Prepositions and Nouns—III

Note the following use of nouns followed by prepositions. Both the prepositions and nouns governed by them are written in italics. Other prepositions have been given in bold.

1. She has great *ability for* (or *in*) office work.
2. He observes complete *abstinence from* wine.
3. I have no *access to* the Chief Minister.
4. *Access to* the cave/peak was difficult.
5. He was arrested **under** the *accusation of* theft.
6. A mother has a great *affection for* her child.
7. His *allusion to* Macaulay was natural.
8. He has no *ambition for* being a billionaire.
9. There is no *alternative to* this remedy **for** small-pox.
10. *Alternation of* day **with** night is a natural phenomenon.
11. Have you made any *alteration in* your plan?
12. You will have **to** make *amends for* this loss.
13. I have no *animosity against* him.
14. What is the *antidote to* this poison.
15. He showed great *anxiety for* the safety **of** his son.
16. I have no *appetite for* food.
17. He has a great *aptitude for* biology.
18. Have you submitted your *application for* the position **of** manager.
19. He has shown a great *concern for* this matter.

20. I give you full *assurance of* (my) help.

21. Has the President given his *assent to* the Bill.

22. Animals behave strangely **on** *apprehension of* danger.

23. You should pay full *attention to* your study/studies.

24. I have full *authority over* my subordinates.

25. He entered into a *bargain with* me **for** the purchase of the house.

26. Many people suffer **from** *blindness to* their own faults.

27. He has a great *capacity for* hard work.

28. It is, indeed, a *cause for* anxiety.

29. We must observe all *cautions against* making mistakes **in** life.

30. Has the *cessation of* hostilities been declared **by** the warring countries?

31. Please take *care of* your health.

32. I can easily give a *certificate of* good conduct **to** him.

33. He was held **under** *the charge of* murder.

34. His *collusion with* antisocial elements has been proved.

35. He is no *match for* you.

36. I have received a *complaint against* you.

37. There can be no *comparison between* a horse and a donkey.

38. An ass cannot stand in *comparison with* a horse.

39. Will you like **to** give some *comments on* this matter?

40. You 'll have **to** pay adequate *compensation for* causing/ making this *loss to* the company/government.

41. He has shown his full *concurrence with* me **in** this matter.

42. I have full *confidence in* you.

43. One has to work **in** *conformity with* the prevailing customs.
44. I have no *connection with* him/this matter.
45. Ben Jonson was a *contemporary of* Shakespeare.
46. I have a great *contempt for* him/the institution **of** dowry.
47. He is a *contrast to* his brother.
48. Have you sent/made your *contribution to* the PM's National Relief Fund?
49. I have no *control over* him.
50. I had a long *conversation with* him.
51. She took great *delight in* teasing others.
52. His total *dependence on* you is not desirable.
53. He is a *disgrace to* his family.
54. She has a great *craving for* a life of luxury.
55. He has a great *desire for* wealth/riches.
56. We can't allow any *deviation from* the universally accepted *rules of* morality/ethics.
57. Fielding makes several *degressions from* the main story **of** Tom Jones.
58. I'm **in** total *disagreement with* you **in** this matter.
59. Aurangzeb showed his total *dislike to* his brother, Dara.
60. I have a *distaste for* music.
61. I have no *doubt about* his honesty.
62. Is there any *understanding between* you and him **about/in** this matter?
63. A *thought of* the devil brings the devil instantaneously.
64. Simple *trust in* God can work wonders.
65. You owe an *explanation to* me **for** this *lapse on* your part.

66. We should be conscious **of** our *duty/duties to/towards* the country.

67. He is full **of** *eagerness for* fame.

68. We should be *conscious of* the *value of* economy **of** time.

69. He has gained a great *eminence in* singing.

70. It is an *encroachment on* the human *rights of* the common people.

71. I have no *enmity with* him.

72. His *demand for equality with* you **in** the *matter of* rank/wages is not unjust.

73. There is no *escape from* the situation/punishment.

74. *Evasion of* tax/excise duty must be checked.

75. Can you cite any *exception to* this rule?

76. *Ignorance of* law is no *excuse for* violating it.

77. There can be no *excuse for* fault.

78. Small scale industries have got an *exemption from* duty.

79. He has no *experience of* the *life of* a hunter.

80. I have a great *esteem/regard for* him.

81. I have full *faith in* him.

82. I have no *familiarity with* him/ such *type of* business.

83. You will have to pay a *fine for* your being absent **from** school.

84. He has great *fondness for* music.

85. Let us have *freedom from* want.

86. She has a *genius for* science

87. She is a *genius in* Botany.

88. She cast a *cold glance at* me.

89. I am ready to give a *guarantee for* his honesty.

90. He has *hatred for* dishonest people.

91. Who is the *heir to* your property?

92. Your lazy nature is a *hindrance to* your *progress in* life.

93. Your *lack of* sense is an *impediment to* your understanding things properly.

94. His *implication in* the heinous crime has been proved.

95. The *imposition of* new *taxes on* industry has been widely condemned.

96. New *incentives to* industry have been given **in** the budget.

97. He has no *inclination for* a luxurious life.

98. Your *indifference to* all wordly affairs is stoic **in** nature.

99. What is your *inference from* all what you have heard?

100. Your *indulgence in* wine is deplorable.

101. I have no *influence over* him.

102. I have no *inkling of* the matter.

103. The new machine is an *improvement on* its earlier version.

104. He has a great *insight into* human character/psychology.

105. The police is going to hold an *inquiry into* the matter.

106. I have no *interest in* studies.

107. I have no *intimacy with* him.

108. I have sent an *invitation to* all my friends **to** dinner.

109. This court has no *jurisdiction over* criminal cases.

110. There can be no *justification for/of* such type **of** behaviour.

111. *Laxity in* morals is not tolerated anywhere.

112. Mr. Prashant gave a long *lecture on* "Bringing up

Healthy Children."

113. Many poor people in India have no *leisure for* amusement/entertainment/recreation.

114. A corrupt leader is a *liability to* our nation.

115. I have no *liking fo*r sychophants.

116. There is a *limit to* everything/*to* my toleration/*power of* toleration

117. She has no *longing for* riches.

118. He has a great *lust for* money.

119. I have *malice towards* none.

120. He died a *martyr to* a noble cause.

121. What is the *motive behind* your such an action?

122. There is no *necessity of* going there.

123. Are you in *need of* an assistant?

124. *Neglect of* duty is not permissible **in** this concern.

125. He has a great *nerve for* doing adventurous jobs.

126. His *nomination* to the post has been approved/confirmed **by** the higher authorities.

127. *Obedience to* the Supreme Court's orders is mandatory.

128. What is your *objection to* this proposal?

129. You're **under** no *obligation to* buy this book.

130. The broken bullock-cart in the middle of the road caused a great *obstruction to* the traffic/**to** the *movement of* vehicles **on** the road.

131. Adultery is not only a crime but also an *offence against* morality.

132. It is a rare opportunity for you to make a remarkable *progresss in* life.

133. I have placed an *order for* books **with** a leading book-

seller of the town.

134. I had *parleys with* him **for** a long time.

135. He has a *passion for* niceties.

136. Your *partnership with* him **in** this concern is commendable.

137. India is **at** *peace with* all her neighbours.

138. She had to go **for** a long *penance for* having committed adultery.

139. We should show mercy to the neglected and forsaken.

140. He got a great *popularity with* his countrymen **for** his noble deeds.

141. Did you write a *postscript to* the latter **to** your uncle?

142. She takes *pride in* her beauty.

143. I have no *prejudice against* anybody.

144. You must take all *precautions against* Cholera.

145. Who wrote the *preface to* your book?

146. America's ostensible *concern for* human rights is just a *pretension for interference/interfering in* other countries affairs.

147. He has got full *proficiency in* speaking Spanish.

148. Some people have an unmitigable *propensity for* eating.

149. The workers held a demonstration/protest rally **against** the *policy of* privatization/globalization.

150. He has got all the necessary *qualifications for* this office.

151. What is the *point at* issue?

152. What is the *cause of* quarrel?

153. It is a *cause for* concern.

154. Can you give any *reason for* your *absence from* the

meeting?

155. I want full *remuneration/recompense for* my labour.

156. You recent conduct is a *reflection on* your honesty.

157. I have great *regard for* others' sentiments/feelings.

158. Is there any *remedy for/against* snake-bite?

159. Have you sent a *reply to* your uncle's letter?

160. He has got a great *reputation for* his truthfulness.

161. This pen bears *resemblance to* that.

162. Have you got any *relief from* pain?

163. Jehangir raised the *banner of* revolt **against** Akbar.

164. He is my *rival/competitor in* the *business of* textile manufacturing.

165. I have no *rivalry with* him.

166. Ben Jonson wrote wonderful *satires against* human follies and foibles.

167. He is in *search for* gold.

168. He went out in *search of* truth.

169. Immorality is a *sin against* God.

170. He is a *slave to* greed.

171. This evil deed is a *slur on* his fair name/character.

172. Complete *submission to* the will **of** God is essential **for** every theist.

173. A daily *dose of* vitamin pills is a *supplement to* your normal diet.

174. I am ready to stand *surety for* him.

175. I am in full *sympathy with* the tsunami victims.

176. As he joined the services, he had the first *taste of* an arduous life.

177. I have no *taste for* gardening.

178. His fair and square dealings bear *testimony to* his honesty.

179. Jai Chand proved a *traitor to* the country.

180. I have lost my *power of tolerance/over* him/*over* ill-temper.

181. He has written a *treatise on* yoga.

182. *To* what *use* will you put this machine?

183. Your *findings in* the matter are at *variance with* your friend's.

184. I am at *variance with* you **in** this matter.

185. She fell a *victim to* circumstances.

186. His scheme fell through for *want/paucity* of funds.

187. You can be most successful if you can achieve a *victory over* yourself.

188. The court has issued a non-bailable *warrant for* his arrest.

189. Aurangzeb was witness to the *ruining/ruins of* his own empire.

190. Your *yearning for* a safe sanctuary is but natural.

191. She has a great *zeal/enthusiasm* for work.

192. We must have a *zest for* life.

ॐ

8. PREPOSITIONS ADJECTIVES AND PARTICIPLES

In the following sentences adjectives and participles are followed by prepositions. The concerned prepositions and adjectives and participles are written in bold letters; other prepositions are in Italics—

1. He is **absorbed in** his work.

2. The child was **abandoned to** his fate *by* the kidnappers.

3. Drinking is a **abhorrent to** me.

4. He has been **absolved of** the charge *of* murder.

5. This arrangement is not **acceptable to** me.

6. The shrine is not **accessible to** the devotes *because of* snow.

7. We are all **accountable to** God *for* our actions.

8. She is **accomplished/adept/skilled in** dancing.

9. You are **accountable to** a penny *in* your accounts.

10. I am not a **acquainted with** him.

11. I am no **accustomed to** rising early *in* the morning.

12. He has been **acquitted of** the *charge of* theft.

13. He is **addicted to** gambling.

14. My house is **adjacent to** the post office.

15. I'am **avers to** all *kinds of* flattery.

16. A child is very **affectionate to** its mother.

17. He was much **afflicted at/by** the news *of* his friend's death.

18. He is **afflicted with** paralysis.

19. Are you **afraid of** death/a dog?

20. This pen is **akin to** that.

21. She is **alien to** such **kind of** behaviour.

22. He was **alarmed at** the noise *in* the street.

23. We are all **alive to** the situation.

24. I'm **amazed at** his unbelievable success.

25. He is not **amenable to** reason.

26. Are you **amused at** this joke?

27. This is **tantamount to** saying that all the businessmen are dishonest.

28. He is **angry with** me.

29. He is **angry at** my conduct.

30. Is he **annoyed with** you?

31. We are all **answerable to** God *for* our deeds.

32. He is very **anxious about** your health.

33. She is **anxious for/about** your safety.

34. I'm **appalled at** the miserable condition *of* slum-dwellers.

35. This rule is not **applicable in** this case.

36. This book will not be **suitable for appearing in** the IAS examination.

37. I'm **apprehensive of** a great *danger from* him.

38. The minister was **arraigned by** the investigating agencies *for* having indulged in corrupt practices.

39. All the items were **arranged in** proper order *in* the function.

40. Aren't you **ashamed of** your conduct.

41. Karim is quite **assiduous in** his studies.

42. I'm **astonished at** his strange behaviour.

43. She is not **averse to** hard work.

44. Are you **aware of** his intentions?

45. He is **backward in** studies.

46. Happiness *in* family is **based on** the principle *of* making small sacrifices *for* each other/one another.

47. In autumn the trees are **bare of** leaves.

48. He has been **blessed with** a son/ a daughter/ good health, etc.

49. Many a blessing has been **bestowed by** God *on* mankind.

50. We should never be **ungrateful to** anybody.

51. I'm **thankful to** you for this help.

52. He was **beguiled into** committing the crime.

53. I'm much **beholden to** you *for* this help.

54. He is **bent on** making mischief.

55. His path was **beset with** difficulties.

56. We should never be **prejudicial in** our attitude.

57. He has an impartial **attitude towards** all.

58. We should never be **bigotted in** our opinion.

59. He is **boastful of** his high lineage.

60. He is **blind of** one eye.

61. He is **blind to** his son's faults.

62. He was **born at** Karimganj *in* Bihar.

63. He was **born of** rich parents.

64. He was **born in** Delhi/India.

65. She was **born on 15**th July **2000** *at* **5.00** a.m.

66. This train is **bound for** Delhi.

67. He is not **careful of** his dress.

68. He is **capable of** doing great deeds.

69. At present he is **engrossed in** his work.

70. I'm **certain of** my success *in* the examination.

71. He is **dressed/clothed in** green.

72. The reward was not **commensurate with** his achievement.

73. I'm **committed to** paying Rs.**100**/- only *for* this watch.

74. A banana is not **comparable to** an apple.

75. This quilt is **composed of** cotton.

76. I'm **concerned at** the shape *of* things.

77. The prisoner was **condemned to** death.

78. The climate *of* Shimla is **conducive to** health.

79. I'm **confident of** getting a thumping majority.

80. He is not **conformable/amenable to** reason.

81. I'm **conscious of** my shortcomings.

82. **Consequent on** the death of his father, he had to work hard to make a living.

83. He was **conspicuous by** his absence *from* the meeting.

84. I'm **contented with** my lot.

85. This action is **contrary to** law.

86. I'm **conversant with** such type *of* machines.

87. I'm **convinced of** his honesty *of* purpose.

88. He was **convicted of/charged with/accused of** murder.

89. He has been **cured of** cholera.

90. His intelligence **coupled with** hard work enabled him *to* reach the heights *of* glory.

91. **On hearing** this account, I was **convulsed with** laughter.

92. We should never be **covetous of** others' wealth.

93. You were **correct in** saying what you said.

94. He was **deaf to** all entreaties *for* mercy.

95. **Defeated by** his enemy, he left the city and retired *into* forests.

96. Your plan is **defective in** several ways.

97. He is **deficient in** sense/energy/wit.

98. She is **proficient in** her work.

99. He is **devoid of** all sense of shame.

100. He is **efficient in** his work.

101. She was **defrauded of** her cash *by* some unknown persons.

102. Smoking is **deleterious/injurious/pernicious to** health.

103. I'm **delighted at** the news.

104. He is **delighted in** causing injury *to* small creatures.

105. She has been **deprived of** all her belongings.

106. Your success *in* the examination is **dependent on** several factors.

107. He is **destitute of** money.

108. Drinking is **detrimental to** health.

109. This pen is **different from** that.

110. Why are you **diffident of** success?

111. She is **disgusted with** life.

112. I'm **disgusted at** your performance *in* the examination.

113. Is he **displeased with** you?

114. I'm **distrustful of** his real motives.

115. He has been **divested of** all official powers.

116. Is he **dull of** understanding?

117. I'm still **doubtful of** success *in* this venture.

118. He had to resign his job **due to** ill health.

119. She is **eligible for** this post.

120. She is **engaged to** Ranjit.

121. Your noble remarks have got **engraved on** my heart/ memory.

122. He is **entitled to** a rich reward *for* his achievement.

123. The whole valley was **enveloped in** (a blanket *of*) mist.

124. She is **envious of** your success.

125. He rose **equal to** the task/occasion.

126. I do not think wealth is **essential to** happiness.

127. He has been **exempted from** (paying) the fine.

128. It is believed that he has been **implicated in** the crime *by* the police.

129. A dog is always **faithful to** its master.

130. Are you **familiar with** German?

131. I'm not *on* **familiar/speaking terms with** him.

132. Agra is **famous for** the Taj Mahal.

133. Tagore is very **famous with** the Indians.

134. He was **fascinated with** the scenery *of* Kashmir.

135. Rains are **favourable to** crops.

136. A sinner is always **fearful of** the consequences *of* his sin.

137. He is quite **fit for** this job.

138. She is **fond of** singing.

139. Your scheme is **fraught with** danger.

140. That book is full **of**/replete **with** errors.

141. This pond is **abounding in** fish.

142. He is **gifted with** a good voice.

143. The market is **glutted with** readymade garments.

144. She is **good at** mathematics, but she is **weak in** English.

145. He was found **guilty of** theft.

146. I'm very **grateful to** you *for* your kindness.

147. He is very **greedy/avaricious of** money/wealth/power/ honour.

148. Gandhiji is **held in** high esteem *by* all.

149. She is quite **honest in** her dealings.

150. I'm quite **hopeful of** success.

151. It was **horrified at** the terrible sight.

152. He has a hostile **attitude towards** me.

153. He is **hostile/inimical to** me.

154. She is **ignorant of** the consequences **of** her action.

155. She is **ill with** fever.

156. Now a days every man is **hankering after** money.

157. Your remarks are **immaterial to** the point *under* discussion.

158. I'll go there **irrespective of** the danger **involved in** it.

159. Rock is **impervious to** water.

160. The atmosphere is **susceptible to** change.

161. He is **insensitive to** others' feelings.

162. I'm much **indebted to** you.

163. It is **incumbent on** you to pay all your taxes.

164. He is **indifferent to** all the vagaries *of* weather.

165. Turmeric is **indigenous to** India.

166. Was she **indignant at** your remarks?

167. He was **infatuated with** her.

168. She is **infected with** scabies.

169. This house is **infested with** rats.

170. Hard work is **indispensable to** success.

171. It is **imperative for** you *to* work hard.

172. I'm not **intimate with** him.

173. I'm **innocent of** the charge *of* theft.

174. I'm not **interested in** such people/dancing.

175. He is **insensible to** shame.

176. He was **intent on** reaching his destination quickly.

177. I'm **inured to** all kinds *of* life.

178. He is **given to** gambling.

179. **Drunk with** power, he is out *to* vex everybody.

180. **Invested with** new powers, he is trying to bully all.

181. He was **coaxed/inveigled into** a new plot.

182. Your answer is **irrelevant to** the question.

183. He is **jealous of** your success.

184. She is **lame of** one leg.

185. He seems to be **lax in** morals.

186. Every man is **liable to** error.

187. He is **lost to** all sense *of* shame.

188. The supply of gas is **limited to** the urban areas only.

189. He was **mad with** anger.

190. Be **mindful of** your p's and q's.

191. **On hearing** this, he was **moved to** tears/**with** pity.

192. It is **natural to** a man to endeavour *for* a comfortable life.

193. He is **neglectful of** the interests *of* the company.

194. He is **negligent in** his work/**of** his duties.

195. We must be **obedient to** our parents and teachers.

196. He is **notorious for** committing robberies.

197. It is **obligatory on** you to fill up your income tax return.

198. He is **oblivious of** the fact that I had once helped him *in* hour of need.

199. I'm **obliged to** you *for* this act *of* kindness.

200. He is **pre-occupied with** his work/**in** doing his work.

201. Rude remarks are **odious to** most *of* the people.

202. He is too **officious** in his demeanour.

203. This matter is **open to** discussed/debate.

204. Your fresh remarks are **contrary to** your earlier remarks.

205. My house is **opposite to** the post office.

206. She was **overcome with** grief *on* hearing *about* the death *of* her mother.

207. Health is **paramount to** everything else.

208. We should not be **partial to** anybody.

209. This disease is **peculiar to** this region.

210. She is very **polite in** her manners.

211. Tagore is very **popular with** his countrymen.

212. Character is **precious to** me *above* everything else.

213. He has been **precluded from** taking part *in* the debate.

214. Tea is **preferable to** coffee.

215. A weak child is **prone to** all kinds *of* diseases.

216. He is **proud of** his wealth/power.

217. She has **qualified for** the job *of* a nurse.

218. He is **quick of** understanding.

219. She is **quick at** figures.

220. Are you **ready for** the journey?

221. Soon he got **reconciled to** his lot.

222. The house was **reduced to** ashes/cinders.

223. He is not **related to** me.
224. I'll do this **regardless/irrespective of** consequences.
225. He is at last **repentant of** his sin.
226. Your remarks are **repugnant to** good taste.
227. Contentment is **requisite to** happiness.
228. He is very **respectful to** his elders.
229. Everybody is **responsible for** his actions.
230. His movements were **restricted to** his own house.
231. He may not be **rich in** money but he is **rich in** noble thoughts.
232. A dead man is **rid of** all the worries *of* life.
233. I'm **shocked at** your rude remarks.
234. This temple is **sacred to** the memory of the great saint.
235. I'm **short of** money these day.
236. He is **sick of** life.
237. The government is **silent/tight lipped about** this matter.
238. This pen is **similar to** that.
239. He is **slow of** hearing.
240. She is **slow at** learning.
241. He is **skillful/well-versed in** his work.
242. I'm **sorry for** causing you so much trouble.
243. She was **startled at** the sight of murder.
244. India was **startled out of** slumber as China suddenly attacked her.
245. I'm **sure of** success.
246. The bill is **subject to** the approval of the President.

247. India has food stocks **sufficient for** five years.

248. This dress is quite **suited to** the occasion.

249. He is **suspicious of** your movements.

250. I'm quite **sympathetic with** the tsunami victims.

251. I was **transported with** joy as I got the happy news.

252. We must be **true to** our convictions.

253. We should be **temperate in** our habits.

254. The stag was **vain of** its beautiful horns.

255. I'm **tired of** this sort *of* life.

256. 'Common' is **synonymous with** 'ordinary'.

257. The last days of Hitler are still **veiled in** mystery.

258. He is **versed/well-versed in** English drama.

259. With the powers **vested in** me by law, I'm **authorized to** do this job.

260. She is **wanting in** sense/common sense/wit.

261. He is **wary of** disclosing his mind *to* you.

262. I'm **weary of** this empty life.

263. Your action is **worthy of** praise.

264. He is very **zealous/enthusiastic/eager for** success.

ೞ ೮೦

9. PREPOSITIONS AND VERBS

The following verbs are followed by prepositions as given below. The verbs and prepositions concerned are written in bold letters. Other prepositions have been italicised in the given sentences:—

1. We must **abide by** the laws *of* our country.
2. This pond **abounds in/with** 'fish'.
3. He has been **absolved of/from** the charge of theft.
4. He **abstains from** meat/alcohol.
5. We should **refrain from** telling lies.
6. He **acceded to** my request.
7. You must **act upon** your uncle's advice.
8. You'll have to **account for** your conduct.
9. I **owe** Rs. 5000/- **to** you.
10. He has been **accused of** theft.
11. She has been **acquitted of** the charge **of** theft.
12. All of us have to **adapt** ourselves **to** our cicrcumstances.
13. We will **adhere to** the plan *under* all circumstances.
14. Your omission **admits of** no excuse.
15. I **agree with** you *in* this matter.
16. He **agreed to** my proposal.
17. The hunter **aimed at** the dove.
18. She **alighted from** the train.
19. This project does not **allow of** any further delay.
20. Day **alternates with** night.

21. He **alluded to** your remarks *in* one *of* his books.
22. He **apologized to** me *for* his misconduct.
23. You must **answer for** your misconduct.
24. He has **appealed to** the High Court *against* the judgement *of* the lower Court.
25. I have **applied to** the manager *for* the position *of* cashier.
26. He **apprised** me **of** the whole situation.
27. I cannot **approve of** such a heinous act.
28. Mr. Verma **arbitrated between** the two brothers *in* the matter of sharing *of* property.
29. Please do not **argue with** him.
30. The train will **arrive at** the station *at* six o'clock.
31. He **aspires after** becoming a tourist guide.
32. I cannot **assent to** your proposal.
33. I'm ready to **associate with** him in the execution *of* this project.
34. Please **attend to** me.
35. Please **heed to** me.
36. Please **lend** your ears **to** me.
37. You'll have to **atone for** your sins.
38. You must avail yourself **of** this opportunity.
39. He **avenged** himself **on** him *for* his father's murder.
40. Recent rise *in* prices is **attributed to** the hike *in* prices *of* petroleum products.
41. Do not **bark at** me *in* this manner.
42. Let us **bask in** the sun.
43. You must **bear with** us *for* our compulsion *to* raise the prices *of* our products.

44. The rain drops were **beating against** the window panes.
45. Do not **beat about** the bush.
46. What will **become of** this orphan?
47. We must **begin** the function *with* this song.
48. Our examinations **begin on** Monday next.
49. Do you **believe in** the existence *of* God?
50. This house **belongs to** me.
51. God has **bestowed** many blessings *on* us.
52. **Beware of** dogs.
53. He **blamed** me **for** all the failures.
54. Do not **boast of** your being so clever.
55. Your remarks **border on** being rude.
56. The syce is **breaking in** the horse.
57. A burglar **broke into** his house last night.
58. He **broke up** the bread *into* small pieces.
59. We'll have to **bring** him **to** book.
60. Many ugly facts have been **brought to** light *by* the press.
61. She **burst into** tears/rage.
62. She is **brooding over** her past life *in* solitude.
63. The schools should not **burden** the children **with** too much homework.
64. He **called on** him last night.
65. He **called at** my house last Sunday.
66. Please **call in** the doctor.
67. She is **canvassing for** votes.
68. Please **comply with** my request.

69. His conduct **calls for** strict action.
70. I do not **care** a fig **for** what he says.
71. You must **catch at** the opportunity.
72. He **cautioned** me **against** danger.
73. He **challenged** him to a public debate *on* the matter.
74. He has been **charged with** murder.
75. The workers are **clamouring for** higher wages.
76. The dates *of* the two interviews **clash with** each other.
77. I **concur with** you *in* this matter.
78. I **came across** a strange fellow during my walk *in* the countryside.
79. He has **come of** age.
80. The total amount **comes to** fifty.
81. How did you **come by** this diamond ring?
82. This type *of* trousers has now **come into** fashion.
83. I won't like to **comment on** this matter.
84. You can **communicate with** your friends and relatives *in* seconds *through* the mobile phone.
85. You must **compensate** me **for** the loss.
86. Nothing **comes of** nothing.
87. You'll have to **compete with** him *in* selling your products.
88. He **complained of** ill treatment at the party.
89. You can't **conceal** the facts **from** me.
90. He **conceded to** my demand *for* more remuneration.
91. The convict has been **condemned to** death.
92. I **condoled with** him *on* the death *of* his father.
93. He has **confessed to** his fault.

94. He **confides** all his secrets **to** me.
95. I **congratulated** him **on** his success *in* the examination.
96. He **consented to** my proposal.
97. This building **consists of** three storeys.
98. He **connives at** the faults *of* his son.
99. He has been **convicted of** theft.
100. I **correspond with** him frequently.
101. Your action does not **correspond to** your expressed views/opinion *in* the matter.
102. You can **bank upon/ count on** my help *in* time *of* need.
103. Everybody **craves for** happiness/money.
104. Please do not **crow over** your defeated rival.
105. He has been **cured of/healed of** cholera.
106. He often **dabbles in** politics.
107. At last wisdom **dawned on** him.
108. He is **dallying with** this idea.
109. He **deals in** sugar.
110. My father **deals with** his customers/clients politely.
111. You are **debarred from/barred from** entering the hall.
112. You must **decide on** this matter immediately.
113. Are you ready to **side with** me *in* this matter?
114. India has **decided against** signing the NPT.
115. England **declared** war **on** Germany.
116. We must **deliberate on** this matter *with* a cool mind.
117. The street has been **deluged with** rain water.
118. This matter **calls for** special attention/treatment.

119. Parents have to **depend on** their children *in* old age.
120. You must **desist from** doing any harm *to* him.
121. I **dissuaded** him **from** going there.
122. He **persists in** going there.
123. You must not **deviate from** rules.
124. They **deprived** the poor widow **of** all her belongings.
125. You can't **deter** me **from** doing this.
126. It **devolves on** you to protect the interests *of* your estate.
127. He **died of** cholera.
128. She **died with** exhaustion/fatigue/overwork.
129. He **died by** violence.
130. I **differ with** you *in* this matter.
131. This pen **differs from** that.
132. You must not **digress from** the main point.
133. He **dilated on** the subject.
134. She **dwelt on** the subject *at* great length.
135. My father's ill health **disabled** me **from** going abroad.
136. I openly **disapprove of** your conduct.
137. The management has **dispensed with** his services.
138. He has **disposed of** his old house.
139. I **dissuaded** him **from** going abroad.
140. She cannot **distinguish** a nightingale **from** a crow.
141. The manager **divested** him **of** all his powers.
142. **Divide** this apple **in** half.
143. **Divide** this apple **into** four parts.
144. Twenty **divides by** five.
145. The boss **domineers over** his subordinates.

146. He is always **dreaming of** great things *in* life.

147. You are **driving at** a very important point.

148. Caustic soda **eats into** aluminium.

149. I **elicited** a lot of useful information **from** him.

150. The lion suddenly **emerged from** *behind* the bush.

151. Please **enlarge on** this subject a bit.

152. He has **enlisted in** the army.

153. He has **entered upon** the career *of* a film star.

154. You are **entitled to** all the perks *under* the rules *of* the company.

155. I **entrusted** him **with** this task.

156. The prisoner **escaped from** jail in a very tactful manner.

157. He **exacts** too much work **from** his servants.

158. She **excels in** painting.

159. Are you ready to **exchange** your pen **for** my pencil?

160. The judge has **exempted/excused** him **from** attending the court in person.

161. The judge has **exonerated** him **from** the charge *of* murder.

162. He is **exulting in** his victory *over* his rival.

163. He **failed in** his first attempt to pass the examination.

164. He **fell in** love *with* her.

165. The guests at once **fell to** eating.

166. The cow **feeds on** grass.

167. We must **fight for** this just cause.

168. He was **filled with** joy *on* getting this happy news.

169. Do not **fish in** troubled waters.

170. He is **flirting with** this idea.

171. At last he **got over** all his difficulties.

172. At last I was able to **get at** all the facts *of* the case.

173. I am **getting on with** him smoothly.

174. She has **got out of** the morass.

175. Please **glance at** this new kind *of* bird.

176. I had to **grapple with** the robbers/difficulties.

177. You must **guard against** evil thoughts.

178. Most of the people **hanker after** riches.

179. What has **happened to** him?

180. I have **heard of** something strange *about* him.

181. Do not **hinder** me **from** going there.

182. Your success **hinges/depends on** your hard work.

183. Always **hope for** the best.

184. She **hides** her feelings **from** others.

185. He is **hoping against** hope.

186. America has **hinted at** her intervention *in* Korea.

187. Have you **heard of** Rajan's marriage *with* Shruti?

188. The mosquitoes were **hovering over** the stagnant water.

189. The leader incited the mobsters to **indulge in** acts *of* violence.

190. The minister was **indicted for** corruption.

191. I **inculcated in** him the importance *of* being dutiful.

192. Don't **encroach upon**/ intrude **on** my solitude.

193. I **inferred from** his statement that things are going **from** bad *to* worse.

194. The police is/are **inquiring into** the matter.

195. She **insisted on** her visiting the zoo.

196. I **inspired** him with new ideas.

197. We should instil noble thoughts **into** the minds *of* young children.
198. Please do not **interfere with** me *in* my work.
199. The two lines **intersect with** each other.
200. She **introduced** John **to** me.
201. I **invited** him **to** dinner.
202. Please do not **jeer at** him.
203. You should not **jump to** any conclusion hastly.
204. Who is **knocking at/on** the door?
205. I **know** nothing **of** him.
206. You are only **labouring under** a misunderstanding.
207. She is **slaving over** her studies.
208. Do not **laugh at** him.
209. **Look at** him.
210. Don't **stare at** me.
211. Yeats **cast** a cold eye **on** life and death.
212. I have **laid** (here) all the facts **before** you.
213. He **laid** me **under** an obligation/ a debt *of* gratitude *by* helping me *in* my hour of need.
214. This road **leads to** Bangalore.
215. She **lives at** Darbhanga.
216. He is **leaning against** a post.
217. It does not **lie in** my power *to* punish anybody.
218. Please **listen to** me.
219. She **longs for** a luxurious life.
220. We should **look after** our old parents.
221. We all **look to** God *for* help.
222. I'll **look into** the matter.

223. He has **made up** his deficiency *in* English.
224. The robbers **made away with** the booty.
225. Have you **made up** your mind?
226. You must **march/move with** the times.
227. I **marvel at** your great capacity *for* work.
228. Don't **meddle with** my affairs.
229. The colour of your shirt does not **match with** that *of* your pants.
230. Let me **meditate on/ponder over** this subject *for* some time.
231. The train **met with** an accident.
232. The government is going to **merge** this bank **with** some other bank.
233. Dr. Faustus **mortgaged** his soul **to** the devil.
234. She is **mourning for** her dead mother.
235. I **object to** this proposal.
236. The surgeon is **operating on** the patient.
237. The Ganga **originates from** Gangotri.
238. She **persisted in** going there.
239. He **provided** me **with** all the information I required.
240. Who will **preside over** the meeting?
241. He **overwhelmed** me **with** his kindness.
242. Will you **participate in** the games?
243. Your remarks **offend against** good taste.
244. He will **officiate** as manager **for** two days only.
245. A miser can **part** company **with** his friend but not *with* money.
246. Let us **partake of** dinner now.
247. This question does not **pertain to** me.

248. You'll have to **pay for** your misdeed.

249. At last he had to **pay through** the nose.

250. The lion **pounced on** the deer.

251. Who **plotted against** you?

252. The two forces are **pitched/arranged against** each other.

253. She is **pining for** her lost friend.

254. Those who **live by** the sword, also **perish by** the sword.

255. He **plunged into** the canal *for* a bath.

256. The teacher **pointed at** me to answer the question.

257. Please **ponder over/on** this matter.

258. I **prefer** tea **to** coffee.

259. I **presented** him **with** a bouquet on his birthday.

260. I **prevailed on** him in the long run.

261. Do not **prevent** me **from** going there.

262. He **prides** himself **on** his victory.

263. Hard work **told/preyed upon** his health.

264. I **prohibited** him **from** smoking.

265. Let us **proceed with** the work in hand.

266. Let us **proceed to** starting the business *in* right earnest.

267. Please do not **provoke** me **to** anger/violence.

268. He was **quivering/quaking/trembling with** fear.

269. I'll **punish** you **for** your mischief.

270. Have you **qualified** yourself **for** the post?

271. He **quoted** a line **from** Shakespeare.

272. Do not **quarrel with** anybody.

273. I truly **reckon on** your help.

274. A man's misdeeds always **recoil on** him.
275. Please **refer to** the question raised *in* my last letter.
276. Let us **rejoice in** our success.
277. They **rejoiced over** their victory.
278. She is still **recovering from** illness.
279. At last he **reconciled to** his lot.
280. He **recoiled from** the horrible sight.
281. She has **lapsed/relapsed into** laziness.
282. This pill will **relieve** you **from** pain.
283. He has been **relieved of** his job.
284. I **reminded** him **of** his duty *to* the nation.
285. Please **translate/render** this passage **into** English.
286. He had to **repent of** his follies.
287. He **reprimanded/scolded** me **for** my mistakes.
288. He **took** me **to** task.
289. He is **revelling in** vicious life.
290. I **revenged** myself **on** him for the wrong done *to* me.
291. The tribesmen have rebelled/revolted **against** the government.
292. He was **robbed of** his watch *in* broad-day light.
293. Ashoka **ruled over** India *for* many years.
294. Many people **run after** exotic things.
295. Please **save/rescue** him **from** the kidnappers/destruction/danger.
296. We should not **scoff at** morality/religion.
297. He is **searching for** his lost dog.
298. I **saw through** his game.
299. Please **send for** the doctor.

300. Now, **set about** your business.
301. He **set upon** me (i.e. attacked me).
302. I have **put by** some money *for* my daughter's education.
303. The officer **sat over** the file.
304. Never **side with** an evil person.
305. I **shudder at** the very idea *of* cruelty/violence.
306. Your action **smacks of** some ulterior motives.
307. He **seized at** the opportunity.
308. Can you **speak on** the benefit of trees?
309. He **speaks** high **of** you.
310. Please do not **stand against** me.
311. I'll always **stand by** you.
312. We'll **set out for/start for** Chennai tomorrow *in* the morning.
313. Never **stoop to meanness**.
314. **Strike at** the iron when it is hot.
315. He **struck** a bargain **with** me.
316. He was **stripped of** all his medals.
317. She had to **struggle against** heavy odds.
318. Will you like to **contribute to** this fund?
319. I **subscribe to** the India Today.
320. At last, he **succeeded in** his efforts.
321. He had to **subsist on** wild herbs *for* two days.
322. The accident victim **succumbed to** his injuries *in* the hospital.
323. Please **supply** me **with** all the articles I require.
324. The enemy **surrendered to** our forces.
325. I **sympathise with** you *in* this matter.
326. She **takes after** her mother.

327. **Take off** your shoes.

328. Never **talk of** this matter in future.

329. Hard work **told upon** his health.

330. They **traded** charges **against** each other.

331. At last, you'll **triumph over/get over** all difficulties/obstacles/odds.

332. She began to **tremble at** the sight of a Leopard.

333. We've **tided over** all losses/difficulties.

334. The children **threw** stones **at** the poor beggar.

335. He **threw** a hint **for** me to catch.

336. Never **trifle with** a man's sentiments/feelings.

337. **Trust in** God.

338. They are **vying with** each other to get the top position *in* the examination.

339. Please **vote for** me.

340. He has **embarked upon** a new venture/plan.

341. I **warned** him **of** danger ahead.

342. Let us **wait for** him.

343. We had to **wait on** the minister *for* two hours.

344. He is **working at** the new machines.

345. I had to **wrestle with** a powerful enemy/robber/thief/adversary.

346. A child is always **yearning for** mother's affection.

347. Never **yield to** any temptation.

 times

10. Prepositions and Adverbs

(A)

Sometimes adverbs are followed by prepositions. Read the following sentences:

1. **Agreeably to** my proposals, the company started a new project.

2. **Amenably to** reason, he changed his way of behaving *with* others.

3. **Compatibly with** the circumstances, he tried to adopt himself to the new way of life.

4. **Fortunately for** him, he was acquitted within a day.

5. **Contentedly with** his lot, he decided not *to* run after money.

6. **Conformably to** the prevailing situation, he accepted all the terms at once.

7. **Independently of** what has already been said, it can be asserted that it is not always that daughters-in-law and not the mothers-in-law are the victims.

8. **Loyally to** our country, we took a vow to defend her at all costs.

9. **Prejudicially to** the interests of the company, the management went on recruiting new staff.

10. **Disproportionately to** his income, he went *on* amassing wealth *through* corrupt means.

11. **Consistently with** his honest life, he refused *to* accept bribe.

12. **Inappropriately to** the occasion, he began to singing a merry song *on* that sad occasion.
13. **Decoratively in** his gaudy dress, he began to walk up and down on the stage.
14. **Irrespectively of** consequences, he jumped into the fray.
15. **Patriotically to** the bone, he laid down his life *for* the country/nation.

(B)

Sometimes, prepositions and adverbs are confused with each others. Read the following examples:

a) In the following sentences, words in bold letters are prepositions :—

   i. I climbed **up** the tree.

   ii. She climbed **down** the stairs.

   iii. We sat **in** the room.

   iv. I'll reach the destination **before** him.

   v. Rains will come **after** summer.

b) In the following sentences, words in bold letters are adverbs:

   i. Stand **up**, please.

   ii. Sit **down**, please.

   iii. Come **in**.

   iv. I've never visited this place **before**.

   v. We look **before** and **after**.

EXERCISE

In the following sentences, please point out whether the word in bold letters is a prepositions or an adverb. Mark a tick against the box [P] for preposition and [A] for adverb. The first one has been done for you:—

1. Go **away**.

   | P | ✗ | | A | ✓ |

2. Come **on**.

   | P | | | A | |

3. Let us go **into** the room.

   | P | | | A | |

4. The cat is sitting **under** the table.

   | P | | | A | |

5. The wheel of the car **came** off.

   | P | | | A | |

6. Let us wait **for** him.

   | P | | | A | |

7. **After** how many days did he return your book?

   | P | | | A | |

8. Look **after** your child.

   | P | | | A | |

9. Don't loiter **about**.

   | P | | | A | |

10. He has never visited this place **since**.

    | P | | | A | |

11. What are you **after**?

    | P | | | A | |

12. He is **about** as good as you.

    | P | | | A | |

13. Tell me something **about** him.

    | P | ✗ | | A | ✓ |

14. **Above** all, he is a good cricketer.

| P | | | A | |

15. Please see the detail (given) **above**.

| P | | | A | |

16. It is **about** to rain.

| P | | | A | |

17. His conduct is **above**-board.

| P | | | A | |

Note : In this sentence, **'above'** actually forms a compound word with **'board'**.

18. Please look **below**.

| P | | | A | |

19. It is **below** my dignity.

| P | | | A | |

20. Never hit **below** the belt.

| P | | | A | |

21. The time which is gone **by** cannot be recalled.

| P | | | A | |

22. He stood **by** me.

| P | | | A | |

23. Oranges are sold **by** the dozen.

| P | | | A | |

24. Prices of articles have gone **down**.

| P | | | A | |

25. I walked **down** the street.

| P | | | A | |

26. She lives **in** Delhi.

P [ ]   A [ ]

27. Such types of pants are **in** again.

P [ ]   A [ ]

28. Don't show **off**.

P [ ]   A [ ]

29. She fell **off** the house.

P [ ]   A [ ]

30. In the new budget, tax **on** cigarettes has been raised.

P [ ]   A [ ]

31. The war is still going **on**.

P [ ]   A [ ]

32. Hurry **on**, please.

P [ ]   A [ ]

33. Please think the matter **over**.

P [ ]   A [ ]

34. Can you jump **over** this high wall?

P [ ]   A [ ]

35. Summer is coming **round** soon.

P [ ]   A [ ]

36. We will go **round** about ten o'clock.

P [ ]   A [ ]

37. Has he got through?

P [ ]   A [ ]

38. He got **up** at once.

<table>
<tr><td>P</td><td></td></tr>
</table>

<table>
<tr><td>A</td><td></td></tr>
</table>

ANSWERS

1. A	2. A	3. P	4. P
5. A	6. P	7. P	8. P
9. A	10. A	11. P	12. A
13. P	14. P	15. A	16. A
17. A	18. A	19. P	20. P
21. A	22. P	23. P	24. A
25. P	26. P	27. A	28. A
29. P	30. P	31. A	32. A
33. A	34. P	35. A	36. P
37. A	38. A		

ೞ ೞ

11. PREPOSITIONS AND CONJUNCTIONS

Sometimes Prepositions are confused with conjunctions. Read the following sentences:

(a) In the following sentences, the words in bold letters are prepositions:

    (i) We'll wait **for** him.

    (ii) We'll stay here **till** five o'clock.

    (iii) She returned home **before** eight o'clock.

    (iv) We reached home **after** sun set.

    (v) I have never seen him **since** the last month.

(b) In the following sentences, the words in bold letters are conjunctions:

    (i) He can't come, **for** he is ill.

    (ii) We'll stay here **till/until** he comes.

    (iii) We must reach home **before** the sun sets.

    (iv) We reached home **after** the sun had set.

    (v) I have never seen him **since** he came here last month.

EXERCISE

In the following sentences point out prepositions and conjunctions. Tick (✓) in 'P' Box for Prepositions or in 'C' Box for Conjunctions. The first one has been done for you.

1. Wait here **until** he returns.

   P ✗   C ✓

2. None **but** him left the meeting.

   P   C

3. It has been raining **since** morning.

   P   C

4. He can't come **since** he is ill.

   P   C

5. Do not put off **till** tomorrow what you can do today.

   P   C

6. **Except** you tell the truth, you can't be let go.

   P   C

7. He came here **after** having finished his work.

   P   C

8. He came here **after** he had finished his work.

   P   C

9. There is somebody outside, **for** I heard a knock.

   P   C

10. He has been working in this office **for** two years.

   P   C

11. Mend your ways **before** it is too late.

| P | |

| C | |

12. Death **before** dishonour.

| P | |

| C | |

ANSWERS

1. C	**2.** P	**3.** P	**4.** C
5. P	**6.** C	**7.** P	**8.** C
9. C	**10.** P	**11.** C	**12.** P

ʚɞ

12. Use of Prepositions as Other Parts of Speech

1. ABOUT

Preposition	:	Do you know anything about him?
Adverb	:	He is about to go.

2. ABOVE

Preposition	:	There is no authority above God.
Adverb	:	We should always look above for help.
Adjective	:	Study the above sentences, please.
Noun	:	We should seek help from above.

3. AFTER

Preposition	:	We should look after our old parents.
Adverb	:	He came here but left soon after.
Conjunction	:	I'll attend to you after I have finished my work.
Adjective	:	An old man often thinks of after life.

4. ACROSS

Preposition	:	We went across the road.
Adverb	:	I'll go across to the post office tomorrow.

5. ALONG

Preposition	:	They walked along the bank of the canal.
Adverb	:	Come along and sit beside me.

6. AROUND

Preposition	:	Do not put your arm around my neck.
Adverb	:	Is there anybody around?

7. BEFORE

Preposition	:	All of us will have to stand before God one day.
Conjunction	:	Think before you speak.
Adverb	:	I had never been to Germany before.

8. BEHIND

Preposition	:	He hid behind a tree.
Adverb	:	We left them behind.
Noun(Colloq)	:	The child slipped and fell on his behind (i.e. buttocks).

9. BELOW

Preposition	:	She is below eighty.
Adverb	:	Please read the sentence five below.

10. BETWEEN

Preposition	:	It is between you and me.
Adverb	:	In this market book shops are few and far between.

11. BEYOND

Preposition	:	What is there beyond space?
Adverb	:	Early Europeans knew nothing about Turkey and countries beyond.

12. BUT

Preposition	:	Who but you can solve this problem?
Conjunction	:	He is honest but poor.

| Adverb | : | You are but a common man. |
| Relative Pronoun | : | There are few but do not recognize the services of Gandhiji to the nation. |

13. BY

| Preposition | : | It was all (done) by myself. |
| Adverb | : | Nobody noticed as she walked by. |

14. DOWN

| Preposition | : | We rowed down the current. |
| Adverb | : | The prices of goods have gone down. |

15. FOR

| Preposition | : | Please stay here for a day more. |
| Conjunction | : | I could not go there for I was ill. |

16. IN

| Preposition | : | I am sitting in the room. |
| Adverb | : | Come in, please. |

17. INSIDE

Preposition	:	Please stay inside the house.
Adverb	:	Why are you looking inside?
Noun	:	The inside of this iron box is rusted.
Adjective	:	Have you read the inside pages of the magazine?

18. LIKE

Preposition	:	He is like his father.
Noun	:	I've never seen the like of him.
Verb	:	What will you like, tea or coffee?
Adjective	:	The twins are very much like.
Adverb	:	He eats like an ogre.

19. OFF

Prepositions	:	He fell off the bicycle
Adverb	:	How were you cut off while telephoning me?
Adjective	:	He lives on the off side (i.e. far) of the garden.

20. ON

Preposition	:	The train is arriving on time.
Adverb	:	Move on, please.

21. OUTSIDE

Preposition	:	Please keep outside the gate.
Noun	:	The outside of this house is very impressive.
Adjective	:	The outside wall of this house needs painting.
Adverb	:	Please go outside.

22. OVER

Preposition	:	Think over this matter again.
Adverb	:	Think it over, please.

23. ROUND

Preposition	:	The earth moves round the sun.
Verb	:	Round up these children, please (i.e. bring them together).
Noun	:	We had a round of the garden ?(i.e. we went round it).
Adjective	:	When was the first Round Table Conference held?
Adverb	:	Have you brought him round?

24. SINCE

Preposition	:	I have never seen him since his marriage.

Conjunction   :   Since you are not ready to help me I cannot take you as my friend.

Adverb   :   He went to Italy last year and has been living there ever since.

25. THAN

Preposition   :   He is happier than me.

(Than here is both a preposition and a conjunction)

Conjunction   :   He is happier than I (am).

26. TILL

Preposition   :   We'll wait for him till five o'clock.

Conjunction   :   Wait here till/until he comes.

Noun   :   Somebody has stolen his till.

(box for keeping money)

Verb   :   The farmers till the land.

27. TO

Preposition   :   I have sent a letter to him.

Adverb   :   Leave the window to.

(*i.e.* do not close it completely).

Particle   :   I want you to do it.

(used in this sense to form infinitives.)

28. THROUGH

Preposition   :   It kept raining through the night.

Adverb   :   He has got through.

29. UNDER

Preposition   :   The rat hid under the table.

Adverb   :   As a result of violent storm, the boat went under.

(i.e. sank under water).

30. UP

Preposition	:	Can you climb up a tree?
Verb	:	He suddenly upped out of the bushes.
Adverb	:	She jumped up with joy on hearing this news.

31. PAST

Preposition	:	It is six past nine now.
Adverb	:	Go past, please.
Noun	:	I know much about his past.
Adjective	:	He has been sad for the past week.

☙ ❧

13. COMPOUND PREPOSITIONS

Some prepositions join to form new prepositions. Examples:

(A)

1. In + to = into

In and into: **In** shows a static position.

Into shows a mobile position. Examples:

In :	We were sitting in the room.
Into :	The child came into the room.

2. Up + to = Upto

Usage : Upto means according to or conforming to some standard. Example

Your behaviour is not upto the mark.

(**Note :** The expression "upto" is usually written in two parts as two separate words : "up to".)

3. Up+on=Upon

Upon and on : On shows a static position; upon shows mobility or movement. Examples :

On :	The book is lying on the table.
Upon :	The dog jumped upon the table.

(B)

The following is the list of some commonly used Compound Prepositions.

1. About	2. Above	3. Amidst	4. Among
5. Amongst	6. Around	7. Before	8. Behind
9. Below	10. Beneath	11. Beside	12. Between

13. Beyond   **14.** Across   **15.** After   **16.** Against

17. Athwart   **18.** Besides   **19.** But   **20.** Upon

21. Over   **22.** within   **23.** Without **24.** Inside

25. Outside   **26.** Underneath **27.** Astride

Explanation : (*also see MacMillian's Grammar by J.C. Nesfield.*)

1. about   =   on + by+out

2. above   =   on + by + up

3. across =   on + cross

4. after   =   of + ter

(It refers to the Comparative of 'of')

5. against =   on + going

6. along   =   on + long

7. amid (or amidst)   =   on + gemang

(it refers to 'in a multitude')

8. around (or round)   = on + round

9. athwart=   on + thwart

10. before =   by + fore

11. behind =   by + hind

12. below   =   by + low

13. beneath=   by + neath

14. beside =   by + side

15. between=   by + twain

16. beyond =   by + yonder

17. astride =   on + stride

(It means "with one leg on each side of" Oxford Advanced Learner's Dictionary)

☙ ❧

14. PREPOSITIONS AS AFFIXES

Some Prepositions help in forming several new words. Some examples are given below:

ABOVE

1. Above-board
2. Above-mentioned
3. Above-named
4. Above-stated

AFTER

1. After-care
2. After-damp
3. After-effect
4. After-glow
5. After-math
6. After-noon
7. After-thought
8. Afterwards
9. Thereafter (i.e. afterwards)
10. Thereinafter (i.e. in that part which follows)

BEFORE

1. Before-hand

BETWEEN

1. Go-between

BY

1. Go-by
2. By-election
3. By-gone
4. By-law (also "bye-law")
5. By-pass
6. By-path
7. By-play
8. By-product
9. By-road
10. By-stander
11. By-way
12. By-word
13. Thereby (It means : by that means or in that connection)

FOR

1. For-as-much-as
2. Forbid
3. Forbear
4. Forget
5. Forgive
6. Forgo
7. Forlorn
8. Forsake
9. Forswear
10. Forward
11. Forwards

IN

(**Note:** In many cases, though not always, the prefix "in" forms an antonym of a word.)

1. Inability (to do a thing)
2. Inaccessible (peak, etc.)
3. Inaccurate (statement)
4. Inaction
5. Inactive
6. Inadequate (supply)
7. Inadmissible
8. Inadvertent (ly)
9. Inalienable (rights)
10. Inanimate (objects)
11. Inapplicable
12. Inappropriate (words)
13. Inarticulate
14. In as much
15. Inattentive (person)
16. Inaudible (voice)
17. Inaugurate
18. Inauspicious (moment, day, etc.)
19. Inborn (qualities, etc.)
20. Inbred (qualities, etc.)
21. Incalculable (harm)
22. Incadescent (giving out light)
23. Incapable (of doing a thing)
24. Incarnation (of God, etc.)
25. Incendiary (causing fire, etc.)
26. Incertitude (uncertainity)

27. Incessant (i.e. continual rain, etc.)
28. Inchoate (i.e. just started)
29. Incinerate (v.) (to burn)
30. Incisive (remarks—sharp and cutting)
31. Incivility (i.e. impoliteness)
32. Inclination (of mind, etc. i.e. slope or slant)
33. Incognito (i.e. concealed or disguised)
34. Incombustible (that cannot be consumed by fire)
35. Income
36. Incoming (calls, etc. against outgoing)
37. Incommensurate (not comparable to......)
38. Incomparable
39. Incompatible (not in harmony with)
40. Incompetent (not competent)
41. Incomplete
42. Incomprehensible (That cannot be understood)
43. Inconclusive (incomplete, not decisive)
44. Incongruous (not in harmony with)
45. Inconsequent (i.e. of no consequence)
46. Inconsiderable (not worth—considering)
47. Inconsiderate (adj) having no regard for feelings of others
48. Inconsolable (that cannot be consoled)
49. Incontestable (that cannot be contested)
50. Incontinent (lacking self-control)
51. Inconvenience
52. Inconvenient
53. Incorporate (verb & adj.)
54. Incorrect

55. Incorrigible (that cannot be corrected)
56. Incredible (that cannot be believed)
57. Incredulous (not believing)
58. Inculcate (v.) (fix firmly in mind)
59. Incurable
60. Incursion (sudden attack)
61. Indebted (owing money, etc., thankful)
62. Indecisive (not decisive)
63. Indefensible (that cannot be defended or justified)
64. Indelible (that cannot be removed or rubbed out)
65. Independent
66. Indescrible
67. Indestructible (that cannot be destroyed)
68. Indeterminate (not determined or fixed)
69. Indifference (disregard)
70. Indifferent (not caring)
71. Indigenous (native)
72. Indigestible (that cannot be digested)
73. Indignity (unworthy treatment)
74. Indirect
75. Indiscipline
76. Indiscreat (not careful or cautious)
77. Indiscriminate (without care or taste)
78. Indispensable (essential)
79. Indisposed (unwell)
80. Indisputable
81. Indistinct (not distinguishable)
82. Indoctrinate (fill a person's mind with specific ideas, etc.)

83. Indoor (as against outdoor)
84. Indubitable
85. Indefatigable (that cannot be tired out)
86. Inedible (not fit for being eaten)
87. Ineffective
88. Ineffectual
89. Inefficient
90. Inelastic
91. Ineligible
92. Inept (absurd in handling a situation etc.)
93. Inequality
94. Inequitable (unjust treatment, distribution of wealth, etc.)
95. Inequity (injustice)
96. Inescapable
97. Inestimable (that cannot be estimated, i.e., too great or precious, etc.)
98. Inevitable (unavoidable)
99. Inexact
100. Inexcusable (that can't be excused)
101. Inexhaustible (that can't be exhausted)
102. Inexorable (not liable to yield)
103. Inexpensive (not expensive)
104. Inexperienced
105. Inexplicable
106. Inexpressible
107. Inextricable
108. Infallible (not liable to make a mistake)
109. Infamous
110. Infancy (abstract noun from infant)

111. Infanticide (killing of an infant)
112. Infantile (showing characteristics of an infant)
113. Infidelity (unfaithfulness)
114. Infidel (one having no faith in religion)
115. Infighting
116. Infiltrate
117. Infinite (not finite)
118. Infinitive
119. Infirm (physically weak)
120. Inflammable (liable to be set on fire easily)
121. Inflate (fill, swell with gas, pride, etc.)
122. Inflexible
123. Inflow(n) (flowing in)
124. Inglorious
125. Ingratitude
126. Inhale (as against exhale)
127. Inharmonious
128. Inhospitable (terrain, etc.)
129. Inimitable (that cannot be imitated)
130. Inhuman
131. Iniquitous
132. Inland (land in the interior of a country, etc.)
133. Inlaws
134. Inlay
135. Inlet
136. Inmate (one of the persons living together in a jail, hospital, orphanage, etc.)
137. Inmost
138. Inner

139. Inoffensive
140. Inoperative
141. Inordinate
142. Inorganic
143. Input (as against output)
144. Insanitary
145. Insatiable (that cannot be satisfied)
146. Insatiate ((one) never satisfied)
147. Inscrutable (mysterious)
148. Insecure
149. Insensate
150. Insensible
151. Insensitive
152. Inseparable
153. Inset
154. Inshore (close to the shore)
155. Inside
156. Insight
157. Insignificant
158. Insincere
159. Insoluble
160. In so much (adv.) (to much a degree or extent-that)
161. Inspire
162. Instability (noun form of unstable)
163. Insufficient
164. Insuperable (not liable to be overcome)
165. Insupportable
166. Insurmountable (that cannot be overcome)
167. Intangible (not capable of being touched or grasped)

168. Intelligible (that can be understood; antonym unintelligible)

169. Intemperate (far from being moderate)

170. Invincible (that cannot be conquered)

171. Inviolable (not liable to be violated, disturbed or disobeyed).

172. Invisible (that cannot be seen)

173. Inaudible (that cannot be heard)

174. Invulnerable (that can't be wounded)

175. Inward

176. Therein (arch.) (i.e., in that place)

177. Therein after (i.e., in the part that follows)

LIKE

1. Likable (adj.) (deserving to be liked; pleasing)

2. Likely (adv.) (It means : seemingly reasonable or suitable)

3. Liken (verb) (It means : to point out likeness between.....)

4. Likeness (n.) It means : resemblance

5. Likewise (adv.) (It means : in the same manner)

6. Liking (n.) (It means : fondness)

OF

1. Thereof (It means : of that or from that source)

OFF

1. Go-off (noun)

(It means 'start')

2. Off-handed (compliment)

ON

1. Onlooker (It means : one who looks on)
2. Onset (It means : vigorous start)
3. Onrush (It means : onward rush)
4. Onslaught (It means : vigorous attack)
5. Onto (preposition) (It means on to)
   (**Note:** The use of 'onto' is mostly made in the USA)
6. Onward (It means forward) (e.g. onward march)
7. Oncoming (It means : approaching)
8. Ongoing (It means : going on)
   (It is not commonly used.)

OVER

Numerous words are formed with the prefix 'over'. Some of them which are more commonly used are given below:

1. Overactive (adj.)
2. Overambitious (adj.)
3. Overanxious (adj.)
4. Overcautious (adj.)
5. Overexertion (n.)
6. Overburden (v.) (e.g. Do not overburden him with work).
7. Overcook/ed (v.)
8. Overeat (v.)
9. Overemphasise (v.)
10. Overestimate (v.)
11. Overheat (v.)
12. Overindulge (v.)
13. Overstrain (v.)
14. Overvalue (v.)

15. Oversleep (v.)
16. Overact (v.)
17. Overall (n.)
18. Overarch (v.) (e.g. Tall trees overarched the canal)
19. Overawe (v.) (It means : to awe completely)
20. Overbalance (v.) (It means : to outweigh)
21. Overbear (v.) (It means : to overcome) (e.g. I overbore his objections through strong arguments)
22. Overbid (v.) (It means : to bid higher than somebody else)
23. Overblown (adj.) (It means : too fully open, e.g. flowers) (e.g. The matter was overblown by the media)
24. Overboard (adv.) (It means : over the side of a ship/board) (e.g., A violent storm threw them overboard)
25. Overcast (adj.) (i.e., for sky covered with clouds)
26. Overcharge(v.) (i.e., to charge price, etc. excessively)
27. Overcoat (n.)
28. Overdo (v.)
29. Overdraft (n.)
30. Overdraw (v.)
31. Overdue (adj.) (It means : beyond the fixed time)
    (e.g. (i) Payment is overdue
    (ii) The train is overdue)
32. Overflow (v.) (i.e., to flow over e.g., the river overflowed its banks)
33. Overgrown (adj.)
    (e.g. The field was overgrown with grass)
34. Overgrowth (n.)
35. Overhand (adj.)
    (used mostly in cricket and swimming)

36. Overhang (v.)

37. Overhaul (v.) and (n.)

38. Overhead (adj.) (e.g., Overhead charges). (also adv.) (e.g. stars overhead)

39. Overhear (v.)

40. Overlap (v.)

41. Overlay (v.)

42. Overlook(v.)

43. Overlord (v.)

44. Overmuch (adj.) (e.g. overmuch work, labour, etc.) (adv.) (e.g. condemned or praised overmuch, etc.)

45. Overnight (adv.) (It means : on the night before)

46. Overpass (n.)

47. Overrate (v.)

48. Overreach (v.)

(**Note** : "Overreach" is followed by a reflexive pronoun)

49. Overrule (v.)

50. Overrun (v.)

51. Oversea (adj.) (e.g., oversea commerce arrangements)

52. Overseas (adv.) (i.e., abroad)

53. Overshadow (v.)

54. Overshoot (v.)

55. Oversight (n)

56. Oversleep (v.)

(**Note** : 'oversleep' is usually followed by a reflexive pronoun.)

57. Overstate (v.)

58. Overstatement (n.) (i.e., exaggeration)

59. Overstay (v.)

60. Overstep (v.)

61. Overstock (v.)

62. Overstruck(adj.) (e.g. overstruck nerves, i.e. strained, tense.)

63. Overstaffed (adj.)

64. Overspill (n.)

65. Overstuffed (adj.) (i.e. thickly padded to make seats, etc. comfortable.)

66. Overtake (v.)

67. Overtax (v.)

68. Overthrow (v.)

69. Overtime (n.) and (adv.)

70. Overtone (n.)

71. Overtop (v.)

72. Overturn (v.)

73. Overweight (n) and (adj.)

74. Overwhelm (v.)

75. Overwork (v.) and (n.)

76. Overwrought (adj.) (i.e., tired out because of excess of work, etc.)

TO

1. Thereto : (It means to that or in addition to that)

UNDER

1. Thereunder (It means :under that)

2. Underhand

3. Underground

4. Underline

5. Understate

6. Understatement

7. Understand
8. Underarm (adj.) (i.e., underhand)
9. Underbid (v.)
10. Underbrush (n.) (It means : undergrowth)
11. Undergrowth (n.)
12. Undercharge (v.)
13. Underclothes (n.)
14. Undercover (adj.) (It means : secret)
15. Undercurrent (n.)
16. Undercut (v.) (i.e., offer goods at a price lower than demanded by others)
17. Underdeveloped (adj.)
18. Underdog (n.)
19. Underdone (adj.) (e.g., meat not completely cooked)
20. Underestimate (v.) and (n.)
21. Underfed (adj.)
22. Undergarment (n.)
23. Underfoot (adv.)

    (It means : under the feet of a person, that is, on the ground)
24. Undergo (v.) (it means : pass through)
25. Undergraduate (n.)
26. Underline (v.)
27. Underling (n.)

    (It means : a person of no importance or position)
28. Undermanned (adj.)
29. Undermentioned (adj.)
30. Undermine (v.)
31. Underneath (adv.) and (prep.)

32. Underpass (n.)
33. Underpay (v.)
34. Underpopulated (adj.)
35. Underpayment (n.)
36. Underprivileged (adj.)
37. Underproduction (n.)
38. Underquote. (v.)
39. Underrate (v.)
40. Undersecretary (n) (i.e., assistant secretary)
41. Undersell (v.) (It means to sell goods at a price lower than others)
42. Undershot (adj.) (e.g., An undershot mill wheel, that is, one worked by water passing under it)
43. Undersigned (adj.)
44. Understock (v.) (as against 'overstock')
45. Undertake (v.)
46. Undertaker (n.)
47. Undertone (n.)
48. Underworld (n.)

    (It refers especially to those living by vice and crime)
49. Underwrite (v.) (It means : to sign an agreement to undertake to bear all the losses, if any)
50. Underwriter (n.) one who underwrites

UP

1. Upbraid (v.) (It means to scold)
2. Upbringing (n.) (It refers to training and education)
3. Upcountry (adj.) = (of or towards interior of a large thinly populated country as Australia or Canada)

    (Examples: a) an upcountry district

b) go or travel upcountry)

4. Upgrade (v.)

5. Upheaval (n.) (It means : great and sudden change characterized by disturbance)

6. Uphold (v.)

7. Uphill (adj.) (e.g., Uphill task)

8. Upholster (v.) (It means to provide seats with covering material, padding, etc.)

9. Upkeep (n.) (i.e., maintenance in a good order)

10. Upland (Often uplands) (n.)

    (It means higher parts of a country or region which may or may not be mountainious or hilly/rocky)

11. Uplift (v.) and (n.)

12. Upliftment (n.)

    (Note : Uplift is more commonly used)

13. Upmost
14. Uppermost They have the same meaning

15. Upper (adj.) (e.g., Upper House i.e., Rajya Sabha, House of Lords, Senate, etc. or upper storey of a building, etc.)

16. Uppish (adj.) (of a self-assertive person)
    (Note: The word is mostly used colloquially)

17. Uppity (adj.) (same as uppish) (eg. I don't like your uppish or uppity behaviour, attitude, etc.)

18. Upright (adj.) and (n.)

19. Uprising (n.) (i.e., revolt)

20. Uproar (n.)

21. Uproarious (adj.)

22. Upsort (v.)

23. Upset (v.)

24. Upshot (n.) (It means outcome or result of some action)

25. Upside-down (adv.)

(It means: (a) the upper side of an object being downwards

(b) not in order)

26. Upstage (adj.) same as uppish or uppity.

27. Upstanding (adj.) (of a person able to stand erect; so it means strong and healthy.)

28. Upstart (n). (a person who suddenly rises to a much higher position in the matter of fame, wealth,power, etc.)

29. Upstream (adv.) (It means : against the current.)

30. Upsurge(n.)

31. Uptake (n.)

32. (a)Up-to-date (adj.) (attributive use)

(b) Uptodate (adj.) (predicative use)

33. Up-to-the-minute (adj.) (It means : latest.)

34. Uptown (adv.)

(It means : in that part of town which is non-commercial, i.e., residential, etc.)

(**Note :** The word is mostly used in the USA)

35. Upturn (n.) (It means a change upwards, that is, a change for the better as in business, etc.)

36. Upward (adj.) (e.g. upward trend)

37. Upwards (adv.)

Examples : (a) Don't turn the bottom of the bottle upwards

(b) Mankind is moving upwards in the matter of evolution/civilization)

UPON

1. Thereupon (It means: Then or as the result of that)

WITH

1. Herewith (It means : with this)
2. Withal (arch) (It means : moreover, as well as)
3. Withdraw
4. Withhold
5. Within
6. Without
7. Withstand (It means : to resist)

15. Use of Prepositions in Phrases, Idioms & Proverbs

Prepositions are used in numerous phrases, idioms and proverbs Some of them are given below:

1. **Between** two stools you fall **to** the ground.
2. **At** arm's length
3. **At** the eleventh hour
4. **In** the long run
5. **On** the run
6. **At** the behest **of**

(**Note:** 'At the behest' of is a phrase preposition. Similar is the case with several other phrases given below.)

7. **In** deep trouble/waters
8. **At** sixes and sevens
9. **Into** the bargain
10. **In** the light **of**
11. To fish **in** troubled waters
12. Think **of** the devil and the devil is there.
13. Account **for**
14. **At** the last moment
15. **At** bay
16. **At** a stone's throw
17. **Over** and **above**

18. **Above** all
19. All **in** all
20. Out **of** sight, out **of** mind
21. **From** the frying pan **into** the fire
22. All **for** (It means strongly **in** favour **of**)
23. All **at** once
24. Free **for** all
25. Add fuel **to** the fire
26. **Beside** the mark
27. A man **of** principle/word/few words/straw
28. **At** the receiving end
29. A jack **of** all trades but master **of** none
30. **Over** head and ears **in** love/debt
31. **Above** the head **of**
32. To hit **below** the belt
33. To beat **about** the bush
34. To labour **under** misunderstanding
35. To put one's back **into**
    (It means : **to** work **at** it **with** strength)
36. To break the back **of**
37. To go **to** the wall
38. To cry **for** the moon
39. To hang **in** the balance
40. **In** the prime **of**
41. The long and short **of**
42. To hanker **after** riches, etc.
43. To beg pardon **of**
44. To show mercy **to**

45. **In** the good books **of**
46. To pay **through** the nose
47. There is a silver lining **in** every cloud.
48. Birds **of** a feather flock together.
49. To kill two birds **with** one stone.
50. To have a bird's eye view **of**
51. To see eye **to** eye **with**
52. A bird **of** prey
53. A beast **of** burden
54. A bird **of** passage
55. A bird **in** hand is worth two **in** the bush.
56. To make a mockery **of**
57. To pay **in** one's own coin.
58. **In** full swing
59. To blaze **with** anger
60. To turn the tables on
61. To be/sail **in** the same boat.
62. To take **to** task
63. To make a clean breast **of**
64. To catch time **by** the forelock.
65. On the brink **of**
66. To bear the brunt **of**
67. To throw dust **into** the eyes **of**
68. To be cut **to** the quick
69. To give a wide berth **to**
70. To deal **with**
71. To deal **in**
72. To get the better **of**
73. **Between** the devil and the deep sea.

74. To abide **by**

75. To knock the bottom out **of**

76. To cast pearls before a swine

EXERCISE (Solved)

Use the following phrases and idioms in sentences of your own and also bold the prepositions.

1. To be **in** the good books **of**

   Ans. I am **in** the good books **of** my teachers.

2. **In** full swing

   Ans. The fair is **in** full swing.

3. **Into** the bargain

   Ans. It is all **into** the bargain.

4. **By** fair means or foul

   Ans. This job must be accomplished **by** fair means or foul.

5. **By** hook or **by** crook

   Ans. He got the work done **by** hook or **by** crook.

6. To beg pardon **of**

   Ans. He begged pardon **of** me **for** having wronged me **in** the past.

7. To fish **in** troubled waters

   Ans. Please don't fish **in** troubled waters.

8. To cry **for** the moon

   Ans. When a beggar wishes **for** a majestic palace, he just cries **for** the moon.

9. **In** the light **of**

   Ans. Please explain the matter **in** the light **of** new facts.

10. Fool **of** the first water

Ans. He is a fool **of** the first water.

11. Chips **of** the same block

Ans. Both the friends are chips **of** the same block.

12. Birds **of** a feather

Ans. Birds **of** a feather flock together.

13. **Between** the devil and the deep sea

Ans. He is surrounded **by** adverse situations **on** both sides. Thus, he is **between** the devil and the deep sea.

14. To hanker **after**

Ans. Most **of** the people hanker **after** riches/position/power.

15. **At** length

Ans. He explained the matter **at** (great) length.

16. **In** the long run

Ans. Honesty pays **in** the long run.

17. Set one's own house **in** order

Ans. You should set your own house **in** order before you criticize others.

18. To cast pearls before swine

Ans. To tell a liar **to** speak the truth is just **to** cast pearls before swine.

19. To hang **in** fire

Ans. The matter has been hanging **in** fire **for** many years.

20. A jack **of** all trades

Ans. He is a jack **of** all trades but master **of** none.

21. **Between** two stools

Ans. **Between** two stools you fall **to** the the ground.

22. **At** arm's length

Ans. Keep the naughty boys **at** arm's length.

23. **At** sixes and sevens

Ans. All the articles were lying **at** sixes and sevens **in** his room.

24. To make neither head nor tail **of**

Ans. I can make neither head nor tail **of** what he says.

25. **In** deep waters

Ans. He is **in** deep waters these days.

26. **Over** head and ears **in**

Ans. He is **over** head and ears **in** debt/love.

27. Labour **of** love

Ans. What I did **for** him was only labour **of** love.

28. **On** the run

Ans. The enemy is **on** the run.

29. **In** rage

Ans. The fashion **of** such trousers is **in** rage these days.

30. **At** the eleventh hour

Ans. My friend saved the child **at** the eleventh hour when it was going **to** fall **into** the canal.

31. **At** the beck and call **of**

Ans. He is always **at** the beck and call **of** his friend.

32. Aim **at**

Ans. He aims **at** becoming a doctor.

33. Ask **for**

Ans. I asked him **for** help.

34. Attend **to**

Ans. Please attend **to** me.

35. Bear **down**

Ans. Akbar bore **down** the rebellion.

36. Break **in**

> **Ans.** The syce broke **in** the horse.

37. Break **into**

> **Ans.** The burglars broke **into** his house last night.

38. Call **in**

> **Ans.** Please call **in** the doctor.

39. **After** one's heart

> **Ans.** This is a book **after** my heart.

40. Add fuel **to** fire

> **Ans.** His remarks added fuel **to** fire.

41. All **in** all

> **Ans.** He is all **in** all **in** this office.

42. Apple **of** one's eye

> **Ans.** He is an apple **of** his parents' eye.

43. Apple **of** discord

> **Ans.** This piece **of** land is an apple **of** discord **between** the two brothers.

44. **At** a discount

> **Ans.** This shopkeeper is selling goods **at** a discount.

45. **At** daggers drawn

> **Ans.** The two countries are **at** daggers drawn **with** each other.

46. **At** home **in**

> **Ans.** She is **at** home **in** English.

47. **At** one's wits' end

> **Ans.** I am **at** my wits' end and do not know what **to** do **in** this matter.

48. **At** the bottom **of**

> **Ans.** I'm trying to know who is **at** the bottom **of** this matter.

49. Bed **of** roses

Ans. Life is not a bed **of** roses.

50. A bird's eye view **of**

Ans. Let me have a bird's eye view **of** the matter.

51. A blessing **in** disguise

Ans. His failure **in** the examination proved a blessing **in** disguise **to** him as he worked hard and passed the same examination **in** the first division the following year.

52. Bank **upon**

Ans. You can easily bank **upon** my help **in** time **of** need.

53. Bring **down** the house

Ans. He brought **down** the house **by** his brilliant performance **at** the function.

54. Bring **to** book

Ans. The police brought the culprit **to** book.

55. Bring home **to**

Ans. The teacher brought home **to** the students the value **of** discipline **in** life.

56. Burn the candle **at** both ends

Ans. He is burning the candle **at** both ends through reckless spending.

57. To play duck and drakes **with**

Ans. He played ducks and drakes **with** his father's property **after** his death.

58. **By** dint **of**

Ans. He attained a high position **by** dint **of** hard work.

59. **By** all means

Ans. I'll help you **by** all means.

60. **By** fits and starts

> **Ans**. He is **in** the habit **of** doing everything **by** fits and starts.

61. **By** leaps and bounds

> **Ans**. India is progressing **by** leaps and bounds.

62. To fall flat **on**

> **Ans**. My advice fell flat **on** him.

63. To lend ears **to**

> **Ans**. Please lend your ears **to** me.

64. Cast a slur **upon**

> **Ans**. His act **of** forgery has cast a slur **upon** the fair name **of** his family.

65. Come **of** age

> **Ans**. She came **of** age yesterday.

66. To have a dig **at**

> **Ans**. During his speech the principal had a dig **at** the shirkers among the staff members.

67. A leap **in** the dark

> **Ans**. Never take a leap **in** the dark.

68. A dog **in** the manger policy

> **Ans**. Some countries are **in** the habit **of** following a dog **in** the manger policy.

69. To be dashed **to** the ground

> **Ans**. All his hopes were dashed **to** the ground.

70. Die **in** harness

> **Ans**. Jawaharlal Nehru died **in** harness.

71. Do **without**

> **Ans**. He cannot do **without** a car.

72. Dance attendance **upon**

Ans. He is always dancing attendance **upon** his boss.

73. Harp **on** the same/old tune

Ans. He is always harping **on** the same/old tune.

74. End **in** smoke/a fiarsco

Ans. All his efforts **to** pass the examination ended **in** smoke/a fiarsco.

75. A fish out **of** water

Ans. Without the company **of** his friend, he was feeling like a fish out **of** water.

76. Fall foul **of**

Ans. The two friends fell foul **of** each other.

77. Feel **at** home

Ans. I am feeling **at** home here.

78. **At** home **in**

Ans. She is **at** home **in** mathematics.

79. Follow **in** the footsteps **of**

Ans. We should try **to** follow **in** the foot steps **of** great men **in** history.

80. **In** the teeth **of**

Ans. The bill was passed **in** the assembly **in** the teeth **of** opposition.

81. Get **into** hot water

Ans. You will only get **into** hot water **by** acting upon his advice.

82. Give a wide berth **to**

Ans. Give a wide berth **to** all the antisocial elements.

83. Give one a piece **of** one's mind

Ans. The teacher had **to** give the naughty student a piece **of** his mind.

84. Go **to** the dogs

    Ans. A country which suffers **from** the menace **of** corruption goes **to** the dogs **in** the long run.

85. Go **through** fire and water

    Ans. The freedom fighters went **through** fire and water **for** the sake **of** freedom **of** the country.

86. Hand **in** glove

    Ans. The two cheats are hand **in** glove **with** each other.

87. **On** foot

    Ans. I went **to** school **on** foot.

88. **By** train

    Ans. I went **to** Delhi **by** train.

89. From head **to** foot

    Ans. He was covered **with** mud **from** head **to** foot.

90. Hit **below** the belt

    Ans. Never hit **below** the belt.

91. **In** black and white

    Ans. Let us have the agreement **in** black and white.

92. **In** keeping **with**

    Ans. Your behaviour **at** the function was not **in** keeping **with** you general nature.

93. **At** loggerheads

    Ans. The two countries are **at** loggerheads over the ownership **of** this island.

94. To jump **to** a conclusion

    Ans. Never jump **to** a conclusion **through** haste.

95. Leave **in** the lurch

    Ans. Never leave your friends **in** the lurch.

96. On the verge **of**

Ans. The old man is **on** the verge **of** death.

97. Once **in** a blue moon

Ans. My uncle comes here only once **in** the blue moon.

98. Of to no avail

Ans. The fox made several efforts **to** get **at** the grapes but **to** no avail. (or but her efforts were **of** no avail).

99. Out **of** the wood

Ans. The doctor says that the patient is now out **of** the wood.

100. From pillar **to** post

Ans. The arts graduates have **to** go **from** pillar **to** post **in** search **of** jobs.

101. To play the second fiddle **to**

Ans. He always plays the second fiddle **to** his boss.

102. To rest on one's oars

Ans. I'm not ready **to** rest on my oars **after** doing post-graduation **in** management.

103. A snake **in** the grass

Ans. Beware **of** him as he is only a snake **in** the grass.

104. To stab **in** the back

Ans. China stabbed India **in** the back **in** 1962.

105. To stand **in** good stead

Ans. His earlier experience stood him **in** good stead **in** the new factory.

106. To see **through**

Ans. I saw **through** his game.

107. To make a clean breast **of**

Ans. He made a clean breast **of** everything.

108. Stand **on** ceremony

    Ans.   Please do not stand **on** ceremony.

109. To take **to** heart

    Ans. She took her father's death **to** heart.

110. The sword **of** Damocles

    Ans. The new retrenchment policy **of** the government is hanging like the sword **of** Damocles **on** the employees.

111. Through thick and thin

    Ans. I'll help you **through** thick and thin.

112. Talk **through** one's hat

    Ans. Nobody likes him because he is always talking **through** his hat.

113. Take the law **into** one's own hands

    Ans. Nobody is allowed **to** take the law **into** his own hands.

114. To be a law **unto** oneself

    Ans. Some people think themselves **to** be a law **unto** themselves.

115. At variance **with**

    Ans. Your fresh remarks are **at** variance **with** your earlier remarks.

116. Under the nose **of**

    Ans. Many clerks take bribe **under** the nose **of** their bosses.

117. Under the thumb **of**

    Ans. The clerk is **under** the thumb **of** his boss.

118. Under a cloud

    Ans. These days his reputation is **under** a cloud.

119. Vie **with**

    Ans. **In** the forest plants often vie **with** each other **to** grow.

120. In the wake **of**

    Ans. Often prices **of** goods rise **in** the wake **of** war.

121. To grease the palm **of**

    Ans. Many people have to grease the palm **of** an official to get their work done.

122. Without rhyme or reason

    Ans. He is often scolding me **without** rhyme or reason.

123. At the zenith

    Ans. His fortunes are **at** the zenith these days.

124. At the nadir

    Ans. His fortunes are **at** the nadir these days.

125. By word **of** mouth

    Ans. The officer has sent the instructions **to** us **by** word **of** mouth.

126. Above all

    Ans. He is wise and handsome. **Above** all, he is truthful.

127. To build castles **in** the air

    Ans. It is **of** no use **to** build castles **in** the air.

128. To lead **to** the altar

    Ans. Ramesh led Promilla **to** the altar.

129. To receive **with** open arms

    Ans. They received us **with** open arms.

130. Behind the scenes

    Ans. We don't know what is happening **behind** the scenes **in** the world **of** politics.

131. In cold blood

    Ans. The trader was killed **by** the robbers **in** cold blood.

132. A bone **of** contention

> **Ans.** Kashmir is a bone **of** contention **between** India and Pakistan.

133. Another feather **in** one's cap

> **Ans.** His success **in** the IAS examination **after** doing post-graduate was another feather **in** his cap.

134. To throw cold water **upon**

> **Ans.** His interference threw cold water **upon** all my plans.

135. To commit **to** memory

> **Ans.** Have you committed this passage **to** memory?

136. To come off **with** flying colours

> **Ans.** He came off **with** flying colours **in** the examination.

137. To show a clean pair **of** heels

> **Ans.** **In** the battle the enemy troops showed a clean pair **of** heels.

138. **In** the doldrums

> **Ans.** After the death **of** his father his business is **in** the doldrums.

139. To live **by** the sword

> **Ans.** Those who live **by** the sword shall die **by** the sword.

140. To keep an eye **on**

> **Ans.** Always keep an eye **on** strangers who visit your home.

141. **In** good faith

> **Ans.** I'm ready to comply **with** your request **in** good faith.

142. To be **on** speaking terms **with**

> **Ans.** They are not **on** speaking terms **with** each other.

143. To turn the tables **on**

    Ans. He tried to disparage me **at** the function but I turned the tables **on** him.

144. For want **of**

    Ans. His plans failed **for** want **of** funds.

145. To fall out **with**

    Ans. The two brothers fell out **with** each other **over** a trifle.

146. To fall **upon**

    Ans. Our troops fell **upon** the enemy suddenly.

147. To steal a march **over**

    Ans. Suresh has stolen a march **over** Naresh **in** studies.

148. A flash **in** the pan

    Ans. His sudden emergence as a novelist was a flash **in** the pan.

149. To carry **off**

    Ans. He carried **off** the first prize.

150. To play **to** the gallery

    Ans. Many leaders play **to** the gallery **in** their speech.

151. To throw down the gauntlet **to**

    Ans. He threw down the gauntlet **to** everybody to have a boxing bout **with** him.

152. To bring grist **to** the mill

    Ans. His polite way **of** talking brought grist **to** the mill **for** him (It means yielded him profits).

153. To meet **with** mishap

    Ans. The poor fellow met **with** mishap **at** the very outset when he suffered heavy losses immediately **after** starting his business.

154. To run **with** the hare and hunt **with** the hounds

Ans. He is so cunning that he always runs **with** the hare and hunts **with** the hounds.

155. To take **to** one's heels

Ans. The thief took **to** his heels when he saw the policeman.

156. Of course

Ans. **Of** course, she is a good girl.

157. In course **of** time

Ans. His small business concern grow **into** a big business house **in** course **of** time.

158. With a high/an iron hand

Ans. Akbar bore down rebellion **with** a high/an iron hand.

159. To be **on** one's high horse

Ans. He is **on** his high horse these days and is trying **to** snub everybody.

160. In a jiffy

Ans. I'll return **in** a jiffy.

161. Cheek **by** jowl

Ans. The two friends sit **in** the class room cheek **by** jowl.

162. To kowtow **to** somebody

Ans. Bureaucrats often kowtow **to** the ministers.

163. To take a leaf out **of** one's book

Ans. We should take a leaf out **of** Gandhiji's book and stick **to** truth **at** all costs.

164. To turn **over** a new leaf

Ans. The culprit has turned **over** a new leaf **in** his life and now become a law-abiding citizen.

165. To make light **of**

> **Ans.** Never make light **of** your parents' advice.

166. To be **on** one's last legs

> **Ans.** This custom is now **on** its last legs.

167. To beard the lion **in** his own den

> **Ans.** It is not within the powers **of** everybody **to** beard the lion **in** his own den.

168. To sail **before** the wind

> **Ans.** Anybody can sail **before** the wind.

169. The long and short **of**

> **Ans.** I have apprised you **of** the long and short **of** it.

170. In the nick **of** time

> **Ans.** I reached the station **in** the nick **of** time when the train was about to depart.

171. In a nutshell

> **Ans.** I have told you the whole story **in** a nutshell.

172. To hit the nail **on** the head

> **Ans.** I hit the nail **on** the head **by** telling whole truth about the matter.

173. A stitch **in** time

> **Ans.** A stitch **in** time saves nine.

174. To lead **by** the nose

> **Ans.** A dictator leads his subjects **by** the nose.

175. Out **of** sorts

> **Ans.** I'm out **of** sorts today.

176. To take **with** a grain **of** salt

> **Ans.** His statement must be taken **with** a grain **of** salt.

177. To be **between** Scylla and Charybaris

    Ans. Being pestered **by** both his neighbours, he is **between** Scylla and Charybaris.

178. To escape **by** the skin **of** one's teeth

    Ans. He had a terrible accident but escaped **by** the skin **of** his teeth.

179. To go/fly off **at** a tangent

    Ans. He was following our course **of** action when suddenly he flew (went) off **at** a tangent.

180. On the tapis

    Ans. The matter **of** your promotion is **on** the tapis.

181. To be **on** tenterhooks

    Ans. As the examinations are approaching, every student is **on** the tenterhooks.

182. A figure **among** ciphers

    Ans. A semi-literate person **among** illiterates is like a figure **among** the ciphers.

183. To take the wind out **of** one's sails

    Ans. The Prime Minister took the wind out **of** the sails **of** the opposition **by** declaring free pension **to** the widows **for** which they were clamouring.

184. To put one' shoulder **to** the wheel

    Ans. If you want to get real success **in** life, you must put your shoulder **to** the wheel.

185. To take full advantage **of**

    Ans. You must take full advantage **of** this opportunity.

186. After all

    Ans. I must help him. **After** all, he is my friend.

187. Take **after**

    Ans. She takes **after** her mother.

188. Bring **out**

    Ans. The publisher has brought **out** a new edition **of** the book.

189. On the other hand

    Ans. He is lazy; **on** the other hand, his brother is very active.

190. At the receiving end

    Ans. **In** this matter, the police is **at** the receiving end.

191. with a heavy heart

    Ans. She heard the news/told about the news **with** a heavy heart.

192. On all fours

    Ans. He sometimes walks **on** all fours to amuse the children.

193. For good

    Ans. He has left India **for** good.

194. For the benefit **of**

    Ans. The government has started this scheme **for** the benefit **of** poor classes.

195. Without saying

    Ans. It goes **without** saying that he is a corrupt man.

196. Without let or hindrance

    Ans. You can meet the new officer **without** (any) let or hindrance.

197. To the bone

    Ans. He is a patriot **to** the bone.

198. Die **by** inches

    Ans. The poor old man died **by** inches.

199. To be full **of**

    Ans. He is full **of** courage.

200. To hold a brief **for**

   Ans. I tell you frankly, I do not hold a brief **for** him.

201. A bolt **from** the blue

   Ans. The news **of** his father's death was a bolt **from** the blue **for** him.

202. Rise up **in** arms **against**

   Ans. A large number **of** people rose up **in** arms **against** the British government **in** 1857.

203. With the least resistance

   Ans. **In** some parts **of** India the British were able **to** conquer the land **with** the least resistance.

204. At the bottom

   Ans. There seems **to** be something wrong **at** the bottom.

205. To be aware **of**/alive **to**

   Ans. We are aware **of**/alive **to** our responsibilities.

206. To go **to** the bad

   Ans. The society has gone **to** the bad.

   (It means : it has become completely immoral)

207. To take the bad **with** the good

   Ans. **In** life, we have **to** take the bad **with** the good.

208. To the bad

   Ans. You have Rs. 100/ **to** the bad.

   [It means : you have lost Rs 100/- in the (business) deal].

(**Note : In** sentences No 206, 207 and 208, 'bad' has been used as a noun).

209. To take the cat out **of** the bag

   Ans. He took the cat out **of** the bag **by** divulging the secret.

210. A cat **among** the pigeons

    Ans. The sudden coming **of** the news has proved a cat **among** the pigeons.

211. To take the bull **by** the horns

    Ans. I'll take the bull **by** the horns and accept the situation bravely.

212. To get out **of** bed **on** the wrong side

    Ans. He got out **of** bed **on** the wrong side today.

    (It means : He remained bad tempered during the day).

213. To carry all **before** oneself

    Ans. He is so smart (or intelligent) that he can carry all **before** himself.

214. To be **on** one's good/best behaviour

    Ans. He is always **on** his good/best behaviour.

    (It means : he always takes care to behave properly).

215. To cross swords **with**

    Ans. He is **in** the habit **of** crossing swords **with** everybody.

    (It means : **in** the habit **of** quarelling...)

216. To put **to** shame

    Ans. The paintings **of** this youth will put **to** shame the works **of** many renowned painters.

217. To give somebody the benefit **of** the doubt

    Ans. The accused was given the benefit **of** the doubt and released.

218. To the top **of** one's bent

    Ans. This is a shirt **to** the top **of** his bent (It means: **to** his heart's desire).

219. To make the best **of** one's time, etc.

Ans. He made the best **of** his time and became a famous writer.

220. To the best **of** knowledge

Ans. I can say this **to** the best **of** my knowledge.

221. Even **at** the best **of** times

Ans. Even **at** the best **of** times India may not reach that level **of** prosperity as America has **at** present.

222. Bit **by** bit

Ans. You should try **to** analyse the situation bit **by** bit.

223. A wolf **in** sheep's clothing

Ans. Beware **of** him. He is a wolf **in** sheep's clothing.

224. To hit the mark **on** the head

Ans. You hit the mark **on** the head when you told the whole truth.

225. To buckle down **to**

Ans. He buckled down **to** work.

(It means: he started **to** work **in** right earnest).

226. The proof **of** the pudding

Ans. The proof **of** the pudding is **in** the eating.

227. To make capital **of**

Ans. Some clever people try to make capital **of** everything that happens **in** society.

228. To put one's cards **on** the table

Ans. Has he put his cards **on** the table?

(i.e, Has he disclosed his plans?)

229. Within an ace **of**

Ans. He was **within** an ace **of** death when he was knocked down **by** a running lorry.

230. To make the acquaintance **of**

    Ans. Will you like to make the acquaintance **of** our new neighbour, Mr Kohli?

231. To have nothing to do **with**

    Ans. I have nothing to do **with** him/this matter.

232. To have nothing to say **in**

    Ans. I have nothing to say **in** this matter.

233. To be cut out **for**

    Ans. He was cut out **for** the occupation **of** a lawyer.

234. Free **for** all

    Ans. There arose a confusion **at** the party and now it was free **for** all.

235. Put **on** the alert

    Ans. **In** the wake **of** terrorist attack, security forces all **over** the capital were put **on** the alert.

236. To be **in** one's true colours

    Ans. He was **in** his true colours when the opportunity was favourable **to** him.

237. **At** the drop **of** a hat

    Ans. The stock market reacts this way or that **at** the drop **of** a hat.

238. Nothing succeeds **like** success

    Ans. It is rightly said that nothing succeeds **like** success.

239. While **in** Rome...

    Ans. While **in** Rome do as the Romans do.

240. To cry **over** spilt milk

    Ans. It is useless to cry over spilt milk.

241. To make a mountain **of** a molehill

Ans. Not much harm has been done. Please don't make a mountain **of** a molehill.

242. Every cock fights best————————

Ans. Every cock fights best **on** his own dung-hill.

243. To be cock **of** the walk (school, etc.)

Ans. This boy is cock **of** the school.

(It means: he dominates all other boys).

244. To give way **to** despair

Ans. Never give way **to** despair.

245. To curb **with** an iron hand

Ans. Corruption can be curbed only **with** an iron hand.

246. To be in **for** some/a trouble

Ans. He is in **for** a/some trouble.

247. **In** sun and shower

Ans. The postman/policeman does his duty **in** sun and shower.

248. A man **of** few words

Ans. Mr Prakash is a man **of** few words.

249. To be a taker **for**

Ans. Is there a/any taker **for** this line **of** action?

250. **On** the eve **of**

Ans. Will you please describe the political situation **in** India **on** the eve **of** Alexander's invasion?

251. To catch time **by** the forelock

Ans. We should try to catch time **by** the forelock.

252. A bit **of** a ——

Ans. He is a bit **of** a writer.

253. To tell **upon**

Ans. Hard work told **upon** his health.

254. **In** defence **of**

Ans. What have you to say **in** defence **of** your action?

255. To be **on** the safe side

Ans. Even if he had one pen, he took another **for** the examination to be **on** the safe side.

256. **In** time **of** need

Ans. A true friend always comes to help **in** time **of** need.

257. To be bowled over **by**

Ans. He was bowled over **by** the revelation **of** new facts **by** his opponent.

(It means : he was made helpless or speechless).

258. **In** fulfillment **of**

Ans. The minister got the overbridge built **on** time **in** fulfillment **of** his promise.

259. To put somebody etc. **under** a boycott

Ans. The people have put this shopkeeper (his shop, etc.) **under** a boycott **for** his dishonest dealings.

260. To be **at** the top **of** the list

Ans. He is **at** the top **of** the list **of** the successful candidates.

261. To break oneself/somebody **of** a habit

Ans. I broke him/myself **of** the bad habit **of** smoking.

262. To be **in** the news

Ans. The occurrence **of** a new scam is **in** the news these days.

263. To be **in** the forefront **of**

Ans. He is **in** the forefront **of** every crusade **for** justice.

264. To break away **from** old habits

Ans. It is not easy **for** a man **to** break away **from** old habits.

265. To break down **from**

Ans. His health broke down **from** hard work.

266. To bring **to** ruin

Ans. His evil habits brought him **to** ruin.

267. A breach **of** trust

Ans. To get back upon one's promise is nothing short **of** a breach **of** trust.

268. Too many irons **in** the fire

Ans. He has too many irons **in** the fire.

269. To break off **in** the middle **of**

Ans. She broke off **in** the middle **of** her speech.

270. To break out **in**

Ans. Cholera has broken out **in** the city.

271. To break **through**

Ans. Suddenly, the sun broke **through** the clouds.

272. To break **with** somebody

Ans. Why have you broken **with** your old friend ?

273. **Without** a break

Ans. It has been raining since morning **without** a break.

274. A break **for**

Ans. There is now going to be a break **for** lunch.

275. To make a departure digression **from**

Ans. Here the novelist has made a departure/digression **from** the main theme **of** the novel.

276. To divide **into**

Ans. The events **in** this novel/drama can be divided **into** a number **of** episodes/parts.

277. To make a fine figure **of**

    Ans. Nature makes a fine figure **of** a man.

278. Break/brust **into** a loud laugh/applause, etc.

    Ans. **On** hearing these words **of** the orator/actor, etc. the audience broke/burst **into** a loud laughter/ applause etc.

279. To be **at** breakfast

    Ans. You'll have to wait for a few minutes as he is **at** the moment **at** breakfast/lunch, etc.

280. To bring down the prices **of**

    Ans. The government should bring down the prices **of** essential commodities.

281. **In** the prime **of**

    Ans. He was cut short **in** the prime **of** his life.

282. To catch the tartar **in**

    Ans. I have caught a tartar **in** him.

283. To bring **to** book

    Ans. The teacher brought him **to** book **for** his carelessness.

284. To hush **up** the matter

    Ans. He being an influential person, the police is trying to hush up the matter.

285. To give **up** the ghost

    Ans. The old man gave **up** the ghost last night.

286. To burst **into**

    Ans. On hearing this news, she burst **into** tears.

287. To have not a short **of** a chance

    Ans. He does not have/haven't got a ghost **of** a chance to win the election.

288. To be **in** one's fate

    Ans. Nobody knows what is there **in** his fate.

289. To call **off** the strike

    Ans. The workers have called **off** the strike.

290. To call **out** somebody the top **of** one's voice

    Ans. He called me out **at** the top **of** his voice.

291. To call **in** question

    Ans. Nobody could call **in** question the honesty **of** Mahatma Gandhi.

292. To have an axe to grind **in** a matter

    Ans. She doesn't have an axe to grind **in** this matter.

293. At stake

    Ans. Vital issues are **at** stake **in** regard **to** the new economic policy **of** the government.

294. To turn **over** a new leaf

    Ans. He has turned **over** a new leaf **in** his life.

295. Out **of** question

    Ans. He is a lazy fellow, his getting **through** the examination is out **of** question.

296. To get rid **of**

    Ans. To get rid **of** a selfish friend is not that easy.

297. To get the wind **of**

    Ans. Have you got the wind **of** his new manoeuvres ?

298. To enlarge **upon**

    Ans. Will you please enlarge **upon** your earlier statement.

299. To hang **by** a thread

    Ans. He is critically ill and his life is hanging **by** a thread.

300. A thorn **in** one's flesh

> **Ans.** My grand success **in** the examination is a thorn **in** his flesh.

301. At the hustings

> **Ans.** Let us see which party emerges victorious **at** the hustings.

302. To all intents and purposes

> **Ans.** **To** all intents and purposes, he is a man **of** wisdom.

303. At sea

> **Ans.** I'm **at** sea **about**/**in** this matter.

304. At a loss

> **Ans.** I'm **at** a loss to know what to do **in** this matter.

305. A man **of** letters/principle/parts/word

> **Ans.** He is a man **of** letters/principle/parts/word.

306. To be torn **between** two words

> **Ans.** **At** present, mankind is torn **between** two words, one **of** despair and one **of** happiness.

307. To play **with** fire

> **Ans.** If you are trying to side **with** the antisocial elements, you are only playing **with** fire.

308. To stoke the fire **of**

> **Ans.** We should never try to stoke the fire **of** communalism.

309. In the air

> **Ans.** It is **in** the air that the new budget will give a fair deal **to** the lower strata **of** society.

310. To do away **with**

> **Ans.** The robbers did away **with** the trader.

311. To care a fig **for**

  Ans. I do not care a fig **for** him/what he said.

312. To make amends **for**

  Ans. You will have to make amends **for** your wrong action.

313. To fly **in** the face **of**

  Ans. The peon flew **in** the face **of** the officer.

314. To go hand **in** hand **with**

  Ans. Our personal and social obligations go hand **in** hand **with** each other.

315. To bear **away**

  Ans. Who bore **away** the maximum number **of** prizes **at** the function ?

316. To blow **out**

  Ans. Blow **out** the candle, please.

Note: Strictly speaking, **'out'** is used only as an adverb or an adverbial particle.

317. To blow **up**

  Ans. The enemy blows **up** the bridge.

318. To call **for**

  Ans. The situation calls **for** quick action.

319. To come **after**

  Ans. Summer comes **after** spring.

320. To come **into** force

  Ans. This law comes **into** force **from** tomorrow.

321. To cry **down**

  Ans. It is not proper to cry **down** the success **of** others.

322. To get **over**

  Ans. He got **over** all his problems **with** courage.

323. To get **on** one's nerves

    Ans. He has got **on** my nerves.

324. To go **against**

    Ans. It goes **against** you not to have attended the meeting.

325. To hold **back**

    Ans. Please don't try to hold **back** the facts.

326. To knock **down**

    Ans. He knocked **down** his adversary.

327. To keep **up** appearances

    Ans. He kept **up** appearances even **after** falling **into** a state **of** abject poverty.

328. To leave **out**

    Ans. Please leave **out** nothing **to** chance.

329. To make **for**

    Ans. The thief made **for** the door **after** committing the theft.

330. To meet **with**

    Ans. The train has met **with** an accident.

331. For a while

    Ans. They took rest **under** a tree **for** a while.

332. In high/low spirits

    Ans. You seem to be **in** high/low spirits today.

333. Hour **after** hour/day **after** day

    Ans. The police kept a close eye **on** the situation hour **after** hour/day **after** day.

334. In general, **in** particular

    Ans. We must respect all elders **in** general and our parents and teachers **in** particular.

335. In store **for**

> **Ans.** Nobody knows what is **in** store **for** him the next moment.

336. To learn **by** rote

> **Ans.** He learnt his lesson **by** rote.

337. In vogue

> **Ans.** This type **of** shirts is much **in** vogue these days.

338. Tit **for** tat

> **Ans.** I do not believe **in** the policy **of** tit **for** tat **in** life.

339. To take **to**

> **Ans.** The bad news is that he has taken **to** smoking.

340. ABC **of**

> **Ans.** I do not know the ABC **of** painting.

341. To give a red carpet reception **to**——

> **Ans.** We gave a red carpet reception **to** our new MD.

342. On the spur **of** the moment

> **Ans.** This idea struck him only **on** the spur **of** the moment.

343. In weal and woe

> **Ans.** I'll stand **by** you **in** weal and woe.

344. The gift **of** the gab

> **Ans.** This man can impress anybody as he has got the gift **of** the gab.

345. To set the Thames **on** fire

> **Ans.** By making new kinds **of** missiles India has set the Thames **on** fire.
>
> (It means: She has made remarkable achievement).

346. To put the cart **before** the horse

    Ans. To offer salary **to** a man even when he has not yet started working is to put the cart **before** the horse.

347. To make a clean breast **of**

    Ans. **At** last, he made a clean breast **of** everything.

348. To wash one's dirty linen **in** public

    Ans. Please don't wash your dirty linen **in** public **by** telling the people all **about** the quarrels **within** your family.

349. To keep the wolf **from** the door

    Ans. The poor fellow is working day and night to keep the wolf **from** the door.

350. To have an old head **on** young shoulders

    Ans. He has an old head **on** young shoulders.

351. A shot **in** the arm

    Ans. The offer **of** a scholarship **by** an overseas company proved a shot **in** his arm.

352. With might and main

    Ans. He was ready **with** might and main to contest the election.

353. To rise **to** one man

    Ans. **At** the time **of** war, all Indians rose **to** one man and protected the country **with** might and man.

354. To let the grass grow **under** one's feet

    Ans. I cannot let the grass grow **under** my feet **during** summer vacation (It means : **to** remain idle).

355. To take stock **of**

    Ans. I'm still taking stock **of** the whole situation.

356. To stand **on** ends

    Ans. His hair stood **on** ends **on** hearing this news.

357. Out **of** spirits

Ans. You seem to be out **of** spirits today.

358. Of one's own accord

Ans. He enlisted **in** the army **of** his own accord.

359. With one accord/voice

Ans. The assembly passed the bill **with** one accord/voice.

360. To settle one's account **with**

Ans. Since he insulted me **in** public I'm determined to settle my account **with** him sooner or later.

361. In quick succession

Ans. He fired three shots **with** his gun **in** quick succession.

362. For a song

Ans. The manuscript **of** Wordsworth's poems was sold **for** a song.

363. On the air

Ans. The President was **on** the air last evening.

(It means : his speech was broadcast **on** the radio).

364. To put one's thinking cap **on**

Ans. He is **at** present putting his thinking cap **on** the matter and as such should not be disturbed.

365. To spill the beans **on**

Ans. She spilled the beans **on** her mother and told her **about** the whole matter.

(It means: revealed everything secret).

366. To come **into** limelight

Ans. He came **into** limelight when he published his second novel.

367. To come **to** grief

Ans. You will have to come **to** grief if you continue **with** your evil machinisations.

368. With one stroke

    Ans. He achieved his main objectives **with** one stroke.

369. In one's heart **of** hearts

    Ans. **In** his heart **of** hearts, he finds himself **at** peace **with** his new circumstances.

370. An ace **in** the hole

    Ans. He kept some funds as an ace **in** the hole to use them **in** case the earlier funds fail to deliver the goods.

Note: "To" is used only as a Particle before the basic forms (present indefinite) of verbs to mark infinitives. As such, it has not been treated as a preposition when it forms infinitives.

೮೩ ೮೦

16. WORDS FOLLOWED BY PREPOSITIONS (WITHOUT SENTENCE)

(A)

NOUNS

Abatement of fever/flood/pain.

Abbreviations of a word, etc.

Ability of/in some work.

Abuse of trust, power, authority, etc.

Abdication of throne, etc.

Abolition of slavery, octroi, etc.

Absitence from flesh/wine.

Abortion of foetus.

Abduction of a person (especially a woman)

Abhorrence of flattery etc.

Abundance/plenty of food/rain.

Abjuration of faith, etc.

Access to (a person or place)

(An) Accompaniment of.

Accession to the throne (of new member) to a political party.

Acquaintance with (a person/thing)

(An) Accomplice in (wrong doing)

Adherence to (a plan, rule, etc.)

(In) accord with

Admission to (an institute, etc.)

(Bring on) accusation of (theft) against (a person)

Affection for

Acme of (one's skill, desires, etc.)

Allegiance to

Acquisition of (assets, etc.)

Affinity with

Administration of (Justice, a dose of medicine)

Alliance with

Adoption of a child by someone.

Advantage over/of

Alternative to

Agenda for (the meeting, discussion)

Allusion to

Ask an alms of (somebody)

Ambition for

(lie in) ambush for (the enemy)

Amends for (a loss, etc.)

Analysis of (something)

Antidote to

Antacedent to

Antonym of (bad is antonym of good)

Antipathy to

(In) anticipation of

Apprehension of (danger,etc.)

Anxiety for

Approach to

Appeal to/for

Aptitude for

(win) applause of (audience)

Arrival at
Arrangement for
Aspiration for/after (fame, etc.)
Assessment of (a situation.)
Assault on (a person/mountain peak, etc.)
(Give) Assent to
(Give) Assistance to (somebody)
Assurance of (help, etc.)
Atonement for (sin, etc.)
Attack against (the government's policy)
(Dance) Attendance on
(Pay) Attention to
Attraction for (person)/of (something)
Authority over (a person etc.) **on** (a subject) **to** (say)
Authorization for (something)
Aversion to
Availability of (funds)
(Strike a) Bargain with (a person) for (anything)
(At the) back of (somebody)
Blot on (one's character)
Betrayal of (a cause, secret, etc.)
Board of (governors etc.)
Battle of (wits)
Beauty of (the Taj)
Breach of (trust, peace)
A burst of (applause)
Candidate for
Call of (one's country)
Capacity for

(Make) Capital of (something)
Cause for (anxiety) of (trouble)
Carrier of (disease)
Case of (embezzlement of funds.)
(Observe) caution against.
Centre of (attraction)
Certainty about (something)
Chance of (a lifetime)
Charge of (murder, etc.)
Circulation of (blood.)
Claim on/against
Clarity of (views)
(At the beck and) call of
Collusion with (a person.)
Comparison with (a person/thing)
Comparison between (two things)
Compassion for
Compensation for
Competition between
Complaint against
Completion of (work)
(In) Compliance with (request, etc.)
Complicity in (a crime, etc.)
Composition of (soil, etc.)
(In) Conformity with (rules) etc.
(In) Concurrence with
(In) Consideration of
Concession to (somebody)
Contemporary of (a person)

Conclusion of (speech, treaty)/from (evidence)

Contempt for

Condensation of (steam to water.)

Contrast to (a person/thing.)

(The) Conflict between (employers and employees.)

Community of (workers/peasants)

Coming of (spring)

Class of (students)

Contribution to

Classification of (something)

Control over (a person/situation.)

Control over (Towards the) close of 20th century

Conversation with

Containment of (some/something evil.)

Craving/yearing/longing/wish/desire for

Codification of (some language.)

Collection of (stamps, coins)

(In) Deference to

Dealings with

(Take) delight in

(The) Decay of (teeth).

Deliverance/freedom/riddance from

(In) default of

Dependence on

(A high) degree of (excellence)

Descent from (ancestors)

Demand for (goods)

Deviation from

Demonstration of (a new machine.)

Digression from

Departure from (some old practices.)

Disgrace to

(in the) denomination of

Slur on

Depreciation of (value of assets)

Disposition of (property) (i.e., authority to dispose it of)

Eagerness for.

Ear for (music)

Effacement of (self)

Encroachment on (one's rights, etc.)

Enrichment of (soil, mind)

Endurance of (pain.)

Engagement with (a person)

Engagement in (work, business)

Enmity with

(for the) encouragement of (a person)

Equality with

Eradication of (poverty)

Esacpe from

Esteem for/Regard for

Estrangement from

Evasion of (duty, etc.)

Evolution of (the universe, language etc.)

Exception to (a rule)

Exchange of (goods.)

Excuse for

Exclusion from

Exaggeration of (facts)

Exchange of (views)

Exemption from (duty, penalty, etc.)

Excursion to (the hills)

Experience of/in

Exercise of (mind, brain)

Exposure to

Exhibition of (bad manners)

Failure of (a plan)

Failure in (an examination.)

Federation of (states)

Faith in

Fall from (a high position.)

Familiarity/acquaintance with

Fan of (a star)

Fast for (world peace.)

Tune for

(In) favour of

Fitness for

(For) fear of (life)

Fondness for

Fight to (finish)

Fight for (freedom)

Freedom from (want, care, anxiety, fear)

Flare of (torches, a match)

Genius for

Generation of (heat, electricity).

Glance at (thing or person).

Greediness for

Grief at

Guarantee for

Guard of (honour)

(Be a) guide to (somebody).

(In) harmony with (nature, etc.)

Hail of (bullets)

Hatred of/for

(Under the) heel of

Heir to (throne, property).

Hindrance to

(Throw a) hint at

(In) honour of

Hostility to

Hope of/for (recovery, jam, success)

Ignorance of (a fact).

Identity with/solidarity with

Illusion of (reality)

Immersion into (water, river, canal)

Imprint of (suffering, depriviation etc. on a person's face.)

Impediment to

Imputations on (a person's character)

Implication in

Incarnation of (health, etc.)

Incentive to

Inclination/aptitude for

Indifference to (heat/cold)

Indulgence in (wine, anti-social activities etc.)

Involvement in (antisocial activities)

Infancy of (a nation)

Inkling of

Infiltration into

Inference from

Influence over

Inquiry to (one's reputation.)

Improvement upon.

Insensibility to (pain, beauty, art, etc.)

Insight into

(Get) Inspiration from

Injury into.

Installation of (proceedings of a house, etc.)

Interest in

(To be made the) instrument of (another's crime.)

Interference with (a man's affairs, etc.)

Insurrection against

Interview with

Interlude between (two acts.)

Intimacy with

Interrogation of (an accused.)

Invitation to (tea, lunch, dinner)

(Flotsam) jetsam of (war)

Jurisdiction over.

(Not a) jot of (truth in one's statement)

Justification of/for

Knock of

(A) Knock at (door)

Key to

(A lot of) kick in (something)

Laxity in (morals)

(A) Labour of love.

Leisure for
Lecture on
Leniency to (a person).
Asset/Liability to (a company/country) society.
(In) league with
Likeness to
leg of (the journey)
(First)
Liking for
(A) legion of (soldiers)
Levy of (tax) (Longing for)
(Cast a) Look at (a thing, place, situation)
(A) link in (a chain)
Lust for (money, knowledge, etc.)
(The) long (and short) of
(A) lot of Malice against/towards
Martyr to/for
(A) mandate for /against
Menace to
(The) making of
Motive for/behind
March of (time).
Necessity of/for
(A) native of/nation of
Need for (help)
(In) need of (help)
Neglect of (duty)
Neglect in (doing something)
(Under the) nose of

(In) Obedience to orders of somebody
Objection to
(Place an) order for
Obstruction to (traffic)
Occupation of (premises)
Offence against (morality)
Opportunity for (something/doing something) of (meeting people).
Opposition to
(An) outbreak of (disease, war, hostilities)
Parley/s with (a person etc.)
Paraphrase of (a passage/stanza of poetry)
Partiality for
Position of (the country)
Passion for (cricket, drinking)
(The) Passing of (the year).
(Make one's) peace with (somebody).
(A) pattern of (the virtues).
(At) peace with
(No) Patience with (nosiy people etc.)
Penance for
Paucity of (funds)
Penitence for
(The) penalty for (non-performance/omission to abide by a law/ rule etc.
Perseverance in
Perfection of (detail)
Persistence in
(A) Perversion of (justice, the appetite, etc.)

Popularity with.

Pick of (the bunch) (It means: the best of all of them)

Postscript to (a letter.)

(A) piece of (cloth, etc.)

Precaution against

(A) point for (debate)

Preface to

(A) Platform for (expressing one's views)

Preference for

Popularity of/for

Prejudice against

Portrayal of

Preparation for (an examination, etc.)

Pretext for

Profusion of

Preamble to

(Take) Pride in

(In) Possession of

Progress in

Precursor to

Proneness to (disease, etc.)

(Annual) Precipitation in (place) (That is, fall of rain, snow, etc.)

(In) pursuance of

Preoccupation with

Qualification for

Quarrel with

Query about

Reason for/against

Ramification of (a plot, trade, etc.)
Recompense for
(Be in) raptures over/about (somebody or something)
Reference/allusion to
(At the) rate of
Reflections/Musings on
(within the) reach of
Regard for
(In) regard to
(Grim) realities of (war, flood, famine)
Regret for
Response to
Resemblance between (two things).
Recapitulation of (facts)
Relations with (person).
Receipt of (goods)
Reliance/dependence on
(Give for the Reception of (guests)) reception to
Remedy for/against
Reception after (the wedding ceremony/ cure for)
(A) Recess with (a writing desk and chair in it.)
Remorse for
Recession in (a country, the world etc.)
Repentance for
Reshuffle of (portfolios)
Reply to (a letter)
(A) recipe for (happiness, a fruit cake, etc.)
Repugnance to
Reclamation of (saline land)

Request for

Recognition of (one's services, reality, truth.)

Resignation to (fate, destiny)

Recollection of (facts)

Respect for

Reconciliation between (two friends)

Resistance to (injustice, unjust laws)

Record/s of (events, ancient civilization, moments etc.)

Rebellion/revolt against

Rule of law

Relief from (heat, etc.)

Respite from

Recovery from illness.

Result of (efforts, etc.)

Rectification of (an error)

Rivalry with

Recurrence of (events)

Raverence for

Remission of (fine)

Satire against

Round of (a building)

Rupture with (a friend, etc.)

(To cause the) ruin of

Satisfaction for

(The) sanctities of (the home).

(In) search of /for (gold, truth, etc.)

(Give a) sanction to

(In) quest of/for

(A) sanctuary for (tigers, migratory birds etc.)

Sequel to

(To the) satisfaction of

Sin against (God, heaven)

Saviour of (mankind)

(Have a) Savour of (communalism)

Slave to (an evil habit)

Security from/against (nuclear weapons etc.)

Sorrow for

Selections from (Shakespeare)

Stain on

(To lose) sensation in (one's legs, cross, etc.)

Submission to

(Has the) sentiment of (pity in him).

Subscription to (a magazine, fund)

Settlement of (a dispute between two parties.)

Subsistence on (grass, rice, herbs)

Shape of (things) to come.

Succession to

Share in (property, etc.)

Supplement to

Shock of (one's life)

Supremacy/suzerainty over

Shot in (the arm)

Surety for

Shower of (blows, bullets, rain, hail.)

Sympathy with/for

(To have a great) talent for dancing

Taste for

(Have a) taste of

Test of (one's ability)
Talk of (the town)
Temperance in (food)
(A) tap on (the wisdom) on/at (the door)
Temptation to (something evil)
(Become a) target of (contempt, ridicule, criticism).
(Bear) testimony to
(The) tempo of (production)
Traitor to
Travesty of (facts)
Trust in
(A) test in (English dictation)
Victim to
(wear (A) veneer of (polite society)
Victory over/triumph over
Want of
Witness to
Yearing for
Zeal for (a cause-doing service to others)
Zest for (life, enjoyment).

(B)

ADJECTIVES AND PARTICIPLES

Abounding in/with
Abhorrent to (somebody; to his feelings)
Absolved of
Abominable to (somebody)
Absolved in

Absent from

Acceptable to

Accessible to

Accompanied by

Accomplished in

Accountable to

Accredited to

Accurate in

Accused of

Accustomed to

Acquainted with

Acquisitive of (new ideas, etc.)

Acquitted of

Adapted from

Addicted to (drinking)

Advantageous to

Adequate to (my requirements)

(not) Admissible under (the rules)

Adjacent to (temple)

Adjourned at (time)

Adjourned to (next time, meeting etc.)

Averse to (inflicting pain on animals)

Appropriate to

Affectionate to (mother, parents)

Afflicted with (disease)

Afraid of (death, dog)

Aghast at (a night)

Aggreable to (my wishes)

Akin to

Alarmed at (the news)

Alien to (his nature)

Alienated from (society)

Alive to (the situations/circumstances, prevailing)

Amalgamated with

Amazed at

Ambitions for/of

Amenable to (reason)

Amused at

Analogous to

At (behaviour, etc.) angry with (a person)

Annoyed with (a person)

Annoyed at (behaviour, etc.)

Answerable to

Anxious for/about

Applicable to

Appreciative of

Apprehensive of (danger)

Apprised of (fact, matter)

Approachable to/by

Ashamed of

Approximate to

Assessed at

Apprehensive at (danger)/for (somebody's safety)

Associated with

Assured of

Astonished at

Attentive to

Averse to

Awake to

Aware of

Backward in

Bad for

Based on

(Hands) Begrimed with (dirt, oil, etc.)

Beholden to

Bent on

Benumbed with (cold)

Bereft of

Besieged by

Blessed with

Besmeared with (mud, oil, tar, grease)

Boastful of

Bespattered with (mud)

Born of (parents)

    In (a rich family, India, Delhi)

    At (5.00 a.m. Allahabad)

    on (15th January, 2001)

    in (2001)

Betrothed to

Blind in/of to (one's faults)

Blamed for

(Train) Bound for (Delhi)

(Ship) bound for (America)

Bled to (death)

Busy with (his studies)

Blighted by (constant illness)

Callous to (suffering, appeals for mercy)

Capable of

Careful about (his appearance)

              of (money)

Certain of (success, victory)

Characteristic of (a person)

Charged with (a crime) to (an accounts head) at (a person, animal)

Civil to

Close to (person, one's heart)

Collateral with (something else)

Commemorative of (an event)

Commensurate with

Comparable to/with

Compatible with

Complementary to

Committed to (a cure or course of action)

Common to

Composed of

Controlled by

Close to

Clubbed with Condemned to (death)

Conducive to (health)

Combined with

Confident of (success, victory)

Careful about

Confirmed in (a habit)

Concomitant to

Comformable/amenable to (reason)

Concordant with

Congenial to (one's taste, nature, temperament)
Conscious of (one's drawbacks)
Consequent on
Considerate of
Contented with
Contiguous to
Contrary to
Contingent upon
Conversant with
Convenient with
Convicted of
Convinced of
Conversed with (laughter)
Curious about
Coupled with
Courageous of (him to face the danger)
Covetous of
Crazy on/about (something)
Creditable to
(To be) cross with
Cured of
Crushed under
Deaf to (my entreaties) in/of (one ear)
Decorated with
Deficient in (energy, sense)
Dappled with
Defrauded of (money)
Deadly against
Deleterious/injurious to (health)

Dear to

Dependent on

Deprived of

Derivative of

(e.g., 'Objection' is a derivative of 'object')

    (**Note:** here "derivative has been used as a noun.)

Delayed by (traffic, etc.)

Destined to

Designed for (a special purpose)

Desirous of

Despicable to

Deserving of

Desolated by

Derogatory to (one's reputation, etc.)

Detached from

Detrimental to (health)

Detained for (interrogation)

Devoid of (sense)

Different from

Diffident/confident of (success)

Directed to/against

Disappointed with (a person)

Dipped in

Disgusted with (life)

Disabled for (life)

Disqualified for (a post)

Discriminated against

Distinct from

Dislocated by

Dismissed for
Disintegrated by
Distrustful of (a person)
Disowned by
Divested by
Disproportion to
Due to (illness)
Distressed about
Doubtful of
Ditched by
Dull of (understanding)
Dotted with (trees, houses)
Eager to
Earnest in
Easy of (access)
Eligible for
Economical of (time, energy).
Effusive in (one's gratitude, etc.)
Enamoured with (her)/of (her beauty)
Embittered by (repeated failures)
Endowed with
Eminent for (his virtues, qualities)
Employed in/by
Engaged to (a person) in (an activity)
Enlargement of (heart, intenstines, etc.)
(word) Empty of (meaning)
(object/container) Empty of (contents)
Engraved on (memory)
Endemic of (a place)

Enraged at

Endowed with

Entangled in

Enforceable from (date)

Entitled to

Enveloped in (mist, mystery, controversy)

Enshrouded in (mystery, mist)

Envious of

Equal to (the occasion, task)

Equidistant from

Estranged from

(Get) Even with (a person)

Evicted from (premises)

Exclusive of

Evident to (all)

Exempted from

Exhausted with (overwork, labour)

Exonerated from (blame)

Exposed to (danger)

Expressive of

Faithful to

False to (a friend)

Familiar with (a language, etc.)

Familiar to (a person)

Famous for (learning, knowledge)

Famous with (people)

Fascinated with (person, thing, ideas)

Fastidious about (his food, clothes, etc.)

Fatal to

Fearful of

Favourable to

Fatigued with (the journey, travelling)

Fertile in (resources, inventing new things, excuses, of brain, etc.)

Firm in/of (purpose)

Firm in (his belief)

Fit for

Flooded with (queries)

Flushed with (funds, etc.)

Followed by

Fond of

Foreign to (one's nature)

Forestalled by

Founded on (facts)

Fortunate in

Fraught with (danger)

Frank in (expressing one's opinion)

Free from (blame)

Friendly with

Full of (persons, things)

Frightened by

Gifted with (some ability/abilities)

(Market) Glutted with (commodities.)

Guided by

Guilty of

Hatched by

Healed /cured of

Headed by

Held in (high esteem)
Helpful to (all)
Honest in (his dealings)
Heroic of (him)
Hopeful of (success, victory)
Honoured by
Horrified /Aghast at (sight)
Hostile to
Harmful/hurtful/injurious/detrimental/deleterious to (health)
Identical with
Ignorant of
Ill with (fever)
Illuminated with
Imbued with (confidence, courage)
Impenetrable to (reason)
Imperative for (a person)
Impervious to (water, good advice)
Incidental to
Inconsequent on/upon.
Inclined to
Incongruous with
Incomprehensible to
Inclusive of
Incumbent on
Inconsiderable to
Indebeted to
Independent of
Indicative of
Indifferent to

Indigenous to
Indignant at
Indispensable to (the nation, etc.)
Infatuated with (a person)
Inferior to
Infested with
Informed about/of/against
Inimical to (a person, one's interests)
Intimate with
Inspired with (self confidence, hope)
Insensitive to (touch, feeling, heat, light, cold)
Intimate with
Inured/habituated/accustomed to
Insured against
Involved in
Irrelevant to
Irrespective of (consequences)
Intolerable to
Jealous of
Lame of (one leg)
Lasting for (years , centuries)
Lax in (one's morals)
Liable to (committing errors)
Limited to
Loyal to
Lost to (all sense of shame)
Mad with (anger)
Moved to (tears)
Natural to (a person)

Neglectful of
Negligent of (duty)
Negligent in (one's work)
Notorious for
Obedient to
Obliged to
Meet for
Objectionable to
Obvious of
Observant of
Obstinate in
Occupied in/with
Odious to
Offended with (a person)
Offended at (his behaviour)
Open to (debate)
Opposed to
Opposite to
Overcome with
Overlapping with
Overwhelmed with
Overshadowed by
(mind) Overstrung with (worries, tension).
(Turn) Pale at (the news)
(House) Painted in (red colours, foreground, etc.)
Parallel to
(of) Paramount (importance) to
Partial to
Patronized by

Peculiar to (a person or place)
(Prices) pegged at
Pentinent for (sin, etc.)
(Made) Phenomenal (progress) in view of (the stock market)
Polite in (manners)
Platonic in (his views of love etc.)
Popular with (people)/for (his good nature)
Precious to (a person)
Pompous in (speaking, manners)
Precluded from
Possessive by (nature)
Preferable to
(Give) Preferential treatment to
Prejudicial to
Precious to (me, you)
Preliminary to
Present at (the meeting function, ceremony)
(Holidays) preparatory to (examination)
Prior to
(Be) Prepared for (the worst)
Proficient in
Profound in (meaning)
Proud of
Profuse in (Apologies, thanks, etc.)
Qualified for
Quick of (understanding)
Quick at Botany
Radiant with (joy, smiles, etc.)
Ready for (fight, work, etc.)

Reconciled to (his fate)
Receptive of (good advice)
Red in (tooth and claw) Tennyson
Reduced to (ashes, poverty, etc.)
Regardless of (consequences)
Related to
Relevant to (the subject, point at issue or under discussion)
Relative to (a question, the case etc.)
Repentant of
Replete with
Remote from
Resigned to (his lot/fate)
Respectful to
Responsible for
(Look) ridiculous in (a dress)
Restricted to
Reverse (side) of (a coin)
Rich in (colour, detail, resources)
Revised edition of (a book)
Satiated with
Secluded (oneself) from (society)
Satisfied with
(Show) Scant regard for
Sensitive to (light, heat, cold, feelings)
(Food) seasoned with (spices)
Shocked at
(Resolution) Seconded by
Short of
Secure from/against (attack, danger)

Sick, tired of
Secular in (his views)
Silent about
Secondary to
Similar to
Segregated from
Skilful in
Servile to (public opinion)
Smitten with (recourse)
Sorry for
Sounded about (the matter)
Startled/shocked/alarmed at
Steeped in (poverty, etc.)
Subject to
Subservient to
Sufficient for
Suggestive of
Sure of
Suspicious of
Surprised at
Sympathetic with
Synonymous with
Tricked into/out of
Tantamount to
Troubled by
Trampled under (the feet)
Temperate in (habits)
Torn between (two woulds)
True to

Tilted towards
Useful for
Vein/boastful/proud of
Veiled in
(well) versed in
Vexed at
Wanting in
Wary of
Weary/tired of
Worthy of (praise)
Zealous for

(C)

VERBS

Abet (somebody) in a crime
Abide by (laws, rules, etc.) at/in (a place)/with (somebody)
Abound in/with (fish, etc.)
Absent (oneself) from
Absolve from (a charge, blame, guilt, vow etc.)
Abstain from (flesh, wine etc.)
Abstract (something) from
Accede to/comply with (a request)
Acclimitize to
Accord with
Account for
Act up (on)
Accuse of
Acquaint with
Acquit of

Adapt to (circumstances, etc.)

Add to

Adhere to (a plan, scheme, resolution)

Admit to (a fault)

Agree with (a person)/to (a proposal)

Advert to (something)

Alight from (train etc.)

Advise against (doing something)

Allot to

Agglomerate into (a mass)

Allude/refer to

Allocate to (duties) to (somebody).

Appologise to (person)/for (behaviour, etc.)

Appeal to (person)/against (a judgement)

Alternate with

Apply to (a person)/for (a post)/against (a wrong-doer)

Apprise of (a fact, information)

Analyse the causes of

Approve of

Answer for (wrong doing or guarantee for other's honesty, etc.)

Argue with (a person)/for/against (a point for debate or discussion)

Appear on (the horizon)/in (a meeting examination)/Appear before a court, judge)

Arrive at (a place)/in (a country)

Assemble for (purpose-prayer, etc.)

Assent to

Assign (a task) to (somebody)

Associate with

Assure of

Atone for

Attach to

Attend to

Augur (well) for

Avail oneself of

Award (a medal) to

Awake to (facts, situation, etc.)

Bark at

Back out of

Bank with/upon.

Bask in

Balance (something) on (hand, rose, head, etc.)

Bear with

Bar from (a favour of)

Beg (Pardon) of/(money) of/for (mercy).

Barge into/against (Somebody,something)

Believe in

Beat upon/at (the door)

Beat against (the window – rain)

Beat about (the bush)

Belong to

Bestow on

Bless with

Beware of

Bifurcate into (two parts)

Boast of

Blow out (the candle)

Border on
Blot out (a name, the view, etc.)
Break in (house, etc.)
Break into (a home)
Break with (a person)
Bounce over (the wall, etc.)
Bring (bad name) to
Bring to (book)
Burst into (tears, rage)
Bow to (one's wishes, etc.)
Call on (a person)
Call at (his house)
Call for (close attention)
Canvass for (votes)
Care for (somebody, something)
Care about (doing something)
Catch at (an opportunity)
Carry (something) to excess.
Caution/warn against
Cast off (old, dirty clothes, skin – as snake)
Cater to (somebody's demands)
Cease from (some activity)
Change for (the better)
Charge with (a crime)
Clamour for (wages, rights, etc.)
Clash with
Cling to
Clog (memory) with (useless facts)
Coincide with

Clutch at a straw (as a drowning man)
Come across (meet somebody accidentally)
Come by (a thing)
Come of (age)
Come into (force, fashion, etc.)
Coagulate (blood) with (fear)
Comment on
Collapse under (the weight of something)
Communicate with
Combine with
Compare with (similars)
Compare to (dissimilars)
Come to (one's senses)
Compensate for (a loss)
Compete with (somebody)
Compete in (a race, etc.)
Compete for (a prize, etc.)
Compete against/with (others in trade)
Complain of (something)
Complain against (a person)
Complain to (a person)
Comply with
Conceal (a fact) from
Concede to (a demand)
Concur/agree with (a person)
Condemn (a person) to (death)
Confess to (a fault, crime).
Confide a secret to
Conflict with (of views, etc.)

Congratulate on
Congregate round (a speaker, priest, teacher, preacher)
Connive at
Connect with
Consist of
Conspire against
Consent to
Consort with (one's equals, etc.)
Contend with/against (a person)
Contend for (a thing)
Contrast (one thing) with (another)
Contribute to (a fund)
Converge on
Converse with (a person)
Convert into
Convict (a person) of (a crime)
Convey to
Convince (somebody) of (some fact)
Convey across
Cope with (a person, situation)
Cooperate with
Correspond with (one's needs, words etc.)
(of expenses) to (one's income)
Count on (one's help)
Count (one) among (friends, etc.)
Count from......to...... (as in counting)
Crave for (something)
Cover with/against/from
Cure of (a disease)

Credit (somebody) with
Criticize (somebody) for
Dabble in (politics).
Deliberate on
Dwell on (a subject)
Delegate (rights, powers) to (somebody)
Dawn on (a person)
Demur at (doing something)
Defraud (a person) of (something)
Deliver (a message) to
Deliberate on (a matter)
Delight in
Depend on/upon
Delude (somebody) with (false promises, hopes, etc.)
Deprive of
Depart from (old customs, practices, etc.)
Desist from
Derive from
Despair of (success)
Descend from
Deter (a person) from
Desire for
Deviate from
Detach from
Die through (neglect)
Die of (a disease)
Die in (battle)
Die from (over work, a wound)
Die for (one's country)

Die by (violence)

Detain in (a place, building, etc.)

Detain for (interrogation, inquiries)

Differ with (a person)

Differ from (one thing from the other).

Dilate/dwell/Expatiate (upon a subject)

Detract (attention) from

Disagree with (a person)

Develop into

Disapprove of

Devolve upon

Dispense with

Dictate to

Dispose of

Differentiate (one variety) from (another)

Dispute with

Dip into

Distinguish (one thing) from (another)

Direct to (a place)

Drive at

Disagree with (a person, his views or statement)

Elicit from

Embark upon (on)

Emerge from

Emigrate to

Immigrate into

Encroach on

Endow with

Enlarge on

Enlighten on (a subject)
Enlist in (army)
Entitle to
Entrust with
Eradicate from
Escape from (jail, punishment).
Equip (oneself) for (a task)
Equip (a ship) for (a voyage)
Equip (soldiers with weapons)
Exact from
Exalt to (a high position, rank)
Excel in
Exchange (seats, dresses, etc.) with
Exclude from
Exempt from
Expatiate on (a subject)
Extract from
Exult in (victory)
Exult over (a person)
Fail in (an attempt)
Fall in (bad company)
Fall among (thieves)
Fall in (love with a person)
Fall into (water)
Fall from (the terrace)
Fall on (one's knees, feet)
Fall to (one's lot)
Fall on (evil days)
Feed on (grass)

Feel in (one's pocket/s for money)
Feel along (the wall)
Fish in (troubled waters)
Fight with/against
Get at, over, etc.
Get through (an examination, experience, etc.)
Glance at/over
Give up (one's position to somebody)
Give up (a fortress, etc.)
Give away (prizes)
Grapple with (difficulties, a thief)
Glisten with (tears, dew-drops, etc.)
Grasp at (something)
Grab at (something)
Graduate from (university, etc.)
Hanker after (riches)
Hang (something) from (something)
Heal/cure of (a disease)
Hasten away to (office, etc.)
Harmonize (one thing) with (the other)
Hint at
Hover over
Import into/from
Impress on/with
(Be) Incensed at (somebody's remarks etc.)
Incensed by (somebody's conduct).
Indulge in
Inculcate upon (somebody)
Inculcate in (somebody's mind)

Inculcate in (somebody something)
Infer from
Inform (somebody) of
Inquire into
Ingratiate with (somebody)
Insist on
Insinuate to (somebody something)
Inspire with
Insulate with
Interfere with (a person)
Interfere in (a matter)
Insure against (fire, etc.)
Introduce to
Interdict (somebody) from (doing something)
Intrude on
Interfuse (something) with (something else)
Invite to
Intermingle (one thing) with (the other).
Geer at
Jump at
Keep from
Knock at/on
Know of (somebody)
(known to).
Labour under (a misunderstanding)
Lament for
Laugh at
Lay to (rest)
Lay (stress) on

Lead to

Let (a dog) against (somebody)

Lean against (a wall)

Lean on (a staff)

Leap at (an opportunity)

Lie to (somebody)

Listen to

Load (one's stomach) with (food)

Long/Crave/yearn/wish for

Look after

Look for

Look at

Look through (coloured glasses)

Look over

Make away with

Make for

Make (the best of something)

Marvel at

Meddle with

Mediate between (two persons, countries, etc.)

Merge into

Meet with

Moon away (the time)
    (It means to pass the way aimlessly).

Moralize upon

Muse upon

Mock at (a feeling, etc.)
    (without preposition for a person e.g. he mocked me)

Meditate on/upon

Misconceive of (one's duty)
    (It means : to misunderstand it)
Match with
Merge with
Mourn for
Mix with
Object to
Originate in/from (something)
Originate with/from (somebody)
Occur to
Operate on (a large scale, as of forces, volunteers etc.)
Offend against (taste)
Offend at/by (one's remarks)
Overwhelm with
Part with (money, etc.)
Part (Company) with (somebody)
Part from (a person/persons/one's children/wife etc.)
Partake of
Peer into (a dark corner of the room, etc.)
Peer at (somebody over one's spectacles, etc.)
Participate in
Pay off (one's debts)
Penetrate into
Peep through (a keyhole)
Peep at (somebody from behind curtains, etc.)
Persist in
Persuade (somebody) of (one's sincerity)
Persuade (Somebody) out of (his/her/wrong motives, etc.)
Pertain to

Pin (one's faith) on (somebody)
Pine for
Perish in (an earthquake)
Perish in (an attempt while doing something)
Plot against
Pick out (the side shoots of a plant, etc.)
Ponder over (or on)
Point to (north, ten, one's guilt, wall, door, etc.)
Point out (a mistake)
  (Note: 'out' when used without 'of' is an adverbial particle.)
Present (Something) to (somebody)
Preside at
Prevail on
Prefer (one thing) to (some other)
Prevail over/against
Prevent from
Prey upon
Prick up (one's ears)
Proceed to
Proceed with
Proceed from
Proceed against
Progress in (one's studies, etc.)
Prohibit from
Prompt (somebody) to (be or do something)
Protect from/against
Protest against
Provide for
Provide with

Provide against

Prune away (unwanted growth, etc.)

Pry into (a secret) out of (somebody)

Purge (one's mind) of/from

Puff out of (one's chest with pride, etc.)

Pail at/against

Quote from

Qualify for

Quarrel with

Quake/trouble/shake with (fear)

Race against (time)

Race (the bill) through (the House)

Rebel against

Reason with (a person)

Reckon with

Reckon on

Recompense (one) for

Reconcile with (somebody)

Reconcile (oneself) to (something)

Recover from (illness)

Reel like (a drunken man).

Refrain from (telling lies)

Refer to (something, somebody)

Rejoice over (victory)

Rejoice at (success)

Rejoice in (one's success)

Reflect upon (oneself)

Relapse into (diffidence, idleness, etc.)

Refresh (oneself) with

Relieve of/from (pain)

Regale (oneself) with (a coffee, chocolate, etc.)

Rely on

Remind of

Remove (something, somebody) from

Remonstrate with

Remonstrate against

Repair to (some place)

    (It means: go to or towards)

Reprimand/scold/rebuke for

Revenge (oneself) on

Render into (Hindi)

Respond to

Repent of (folly)

Replaced by/with

Repose (faith, confidence) in (a person)

Report for (duty)

Report to (somebody)

Revel in (vice)

Restore (something) to (somebody)

Revolt/rebel against

Retire (from.....to.....)

Role (a person) of

Retrieve (somebody) from (ruin loss, etc.)

Run after

Return from (some place)

Return to (some place)

Save from

Saunter along (a road street market, etc.)

Search for

Search into

Scrape (the rust) off (something)

Scrape (paint) from (a door, etc.)

See to

See into

Screw up (one's courage)

(that is, to overcome one's fears)

Seek after/for happiness.

Sell off (goods, stock, etc.)

Send for (a doctor)/(somebody) about (his business)

Set about (a business)

Set out (on a journey)

Separate from

Set (the law) at defiance

Set (one's hand) to (a document)

Set (a match) to (old papers, etc.)

Set (something) on (fire)

Set (something) against (something)

Set (a poem, etc.) to (music)

Set up (a memorial, etc.)

Set up (somebody in business, etc.)

Side with (against)

Settle on (for a bird) (a branch of tree)

Sit over

Shine at (an activity, work) etc.

(e.g. Sachin shines at cricket.)

Snack of

Shout at (somebody)

Speculate in (shares)
Sink into (a deep sleep, stupor, a state of depression, etc.)
Stand by/against (a person)
Stand on (ceremony)
Stand on (Prestige)
Skate over (thin ice.)
    (It means to talk about a subject that needs tactful handling)
Stare at (a person)
Stare in (the face, e.g. death)
Skip over (something, an obstacle, brook, etc.)
Skin off (the grease)
Start for
Slow down (the car, the action, etc.)
Strip of (one's powers, authority, etc.)
Snort with (rage)
Struggle against
Speed up (the car, engine etc.)
Speed down (the car, engine etc.)
Submit/yield to
Stalk through (the land as of fame)
Stalk out of (the room)
Stalk along (the road, bank of the river, etc.)
Subscribe to
Stay in (the house, office, bed, etc.)
Stay with (friends, relatives, etc.)
Subsist on
Stick to (one's gun's, plan, etc.)
Stick at (trifles, nothing, etc.)
Stick at (work)
Succumb to

Sting (one) on the nose, cheek, etc.
Surrender/yield to
Stoop with (old age, etc.)
Sympathise with
Strike at (the root of something)
Stuff (oneself) with (food etc.)
Stuff (one's pockets) with
Stuff (somebody) with (evil, foolish ideas)
Stuff (clothes) into (a bag, box, etc.)
Take after
Take (care) of
Take into (confidence)
Take over (the charge)
Take to (heels)
Take to (drinking)
Take upon (oneself)
Travel over
Talk of/about
Talk over
Talk to/with
Tally (of something) with (something)
Temper with
Testify to (somebody's ability, genius, intelligence, etc.)
Taste of (death, salt, sugar, etc.)
    (e.g. The valiant never taste of death but once—Shakespeare)
Tell about (something)
Tell (somebody) from (somebody)
Tell upon
Think of/about
Think over
Thirst for (knowledge, etc.)
Thirst after (revenge)

Tide over (difficulties, losses)
Throb with (excitement—of heart).
Touch upon (a subject)
Thrust into
Tremble at (the sight of a lion)
Thunder at/through/against
Trifle with (others' feelings)
Tower over
Triumph over (obstacles, difficulties one's problems)
Trade in/on/upon
Train for
Trust in
Transfer from.........to.........
View with
Violate (a law) with (impurity)
Want for (somebody)
Warn of
Wait for
Wait at
Wait on/upon
Vote for/against
Wallow in (money, squalor, etc.)
Ward off (a blow, etc.)
Wear down (enemy's power, resistance, etc.)
Wink at
Weigh with/down
Work at/for
Whip up (passions)
Wrestle with
Whistle through (as of wind through the reeds, forest, etc.)
Yearn/long/crave for
Yield to

ॐ

17. Use of Prepositions

EXERCISE-1

Fill in the blanks in the following sentences:

1. Name the major mineral resources ………….. the world.

2. What is meant ……………..external process?

3. Where did we find oldest records ………………….. human activities?

4. Mention the human activities responsible ……. degradation …………biodiversity.

5. Distinguish …………..evergreen forests and deciduous forests.

6. What do you know…….ecosystem?

7. How do natural beauties ……. a place play an important role……. the growth……. tourism based towns?

8. What are the reasons ……. the development ……. permanent settlement?

9. What are tides? How are tides useful ……. us?

10. Peshawar is situated ………………..the Khyber Pass.

11. Invention ……. computer was a big stride ……. development.

12. ……. Northern plains ……. India growth ……. towns was due to favourable climate.

13. The mobile phones helps us to communicate …… anybody ……. any place ……. seconds.

211

14. Leh is the headquarter .... Ladakh.

15. Grasslands are called prairies .... Africa.

16. Earth Summit II was held .... Rio de Janeiro.

17. Sahara is the largest desert .... the world.

18. Name Mid-latitude grasslands .... Australia.

19. Name a forest having trees which shed their leaves ....a part of the year.

20. Name the highest delta .... the world.

21. What do you understand .... Renaissance? What influence did it have .... Europe?

22. Write a short note .... Reformation.

23. Who was Muhammed Ghori? What were his aims .... India?

24. When and why did the Europeans come .... India....... the sea route?

25. Who was the founder....... the Khalsa Panth? Why was it founded?

26. Which were the kingdoms that came .... existence .... the 10th century?

27. Humayun lived .... fifteen years .... exile.

28. Protestant movement was started .... Martin Luther.

29. The second battle of Panipat was fought .... Hemu and Bairam Khan.

30. Which is the holy city .... Muslims?

31. Who was the famous thinker .... the Renaissance period?

32. Give two important functions..................a chief Minister?

33. Why is India divided .... different states and districts?

34. A proposal .... the form .... a Money Bill can be introduced .... the Lok Sabha only.

ANSWERS

1. of	**18.** of
2. by	**19.** during
3. of	**20.** of
4. for, of	**21.** by
5. between	**22.** on
6. about	**23.** in
7. of, in, of	**24.** to, by
8. for, of	**25.** of
9. to	**26.** into, in
10. near	**27.** for, in
11. of, towards	**28.** by
12. In, of, of	**29.** between
13. with, at, in	**30.** of
14. of	**31.** of
15. in	**32.** of
16. in	**33.** into
17. in	**34.** in, of, in

EXERCISE-2

A student lost his Pre-Board examination question paper for Social science. But he wanted to keep a record of it. So he copied some of the question from the question paper of one of his classmates, giving his own question numbers. While doing so, he omitted the Prepositions unwillingly. You are to supply the same wherever necessary, re-writing the sentences. Underline or write in bold letters the prepositions supplied by you:—

1. Give two features .... desert soil.

2. Why is India having a rich variety .... fauna and flora?

3. What are two types .... metallic minerals?

4. Name two north eastern states having .... 60% land area .... forest cover.

5. Give two stages .... resource planning.

6. What are the advantages .... unigauge system?

7. Explain Indian rivers .... the basis .... hydrology.

8. What are the objectives .... planning .... India?

9. What is .... meant favourable balance .... trade?

10. What is meant .... Liberalization?

11. Give the characteristics .... resource.

12. Name two features .... capitalist or free market economy.

13. Why is the conservation .... minerals necessary? Explain three methods .... conservation.

14. Describe the contribution .... South Indian dynasties .... temple architecture.

15. What is meant .... decorate arts? Give three examples.

16. Explain the structure .... consumer courts. How do they function?

17. What efforts have been made .... the Govt. to empower women .... India?

18. What conditions are required .... the growth .... rice and wheat?

19. What is communalism? What factors are responsible .... it?

20. Define globalization. Explain various measures undertaken .... Government of India.

21. Explain how public distribution and fiscal measures help .... controlling price rise.

22. What are the problems faced .... Indian agriculture?

23. The outline map .... India mark the software technology park .... Andhra Pradesh.

ANSWERS

1. Give two features **of** desert soil.

2. Why is India having a rich variety **of** fauna and flora?

3. What are two types **of** metallic minerals?

4. Name two north eastern states having **over** 60% land area **under** forest cover.

5. Give two stages **of** resources planning

6. What are the advantages **of** unigauge system?

7. Explain Indian rivers **on** the basis **of** hydrology.

8. What are the objectives **of** planning **in** India?

9. What is meant **by** favourable balance **of** trade?

10. What is meant **by** liberalization?

11. Give two characteristics **of** resource.

12. Name two characteristics **of** capitalist or free market economy.

13. Why is the conservation **of** minerals necessary? Explain three methods **of** conservation.

14. Describe the contribution of South India dynasties **in** temple architecture.

15. What is meant **by** decorate arts? Give three examples.
16. Explain the structure **of** consumer courts. How do they function?
17. What efforts have been made **by** the Govt to empower women **in** India?
18. What conditions are required **for** the growth **of** rice and wheat?
19. What is communalism? What factors are responsible **for** it?
20. Define globalization. Explain various measures undertaken **by** Govt. **of** India.
21. Explain how public distribution and fiscal measures help **in** controlling price rise.
22. What are the problems faced **by** Indian agriculture?
23. **On** the outline map **of** India mark the Software technology park **in** Andhra Pradesh.

EXERCISE-3

Point out the part of speech of each of the **bold** words in the following sentences and phrases:—

I

1. What is the basic constituent unit **of** living organisms?
2. Name the **solid** part of the earth's crust
3. **Define** density
4. Name any two diseases caused **by** the consumption of polluted water.
5. Why do we sweat a lot **when** the weather is warm?
6. Write two **physical** properties of water.
7. Name any one **aggregation** as lower level of organization.

8. **What** is biotic community?
9. What do you **mean** by a resource?
10. What is the percentage of water that is available **for** use by human beings?

II

1. Why water pipes may burst **during** severe winter?
2. **How** is distilled water prepared?
3. Explain **the** term photosynthesis.
4. What are the factors responsible **for** global warming?
5. Give **two** names of the levels present in between the level of ecosystem and the level of organisms.

III

1. What is eutrophication? State **its** causes?
2. What are the different methods to make water fit for **drinking**?
3. How **will** you show that water is essential for germination of plants?
4. Why is the cellular level referred **to** as the basic unit of lower levels of organisation?

IV

1. The disease bronchitis is caused by **polluted** air.
2. The volume of water **during** solidification.
3. Cells join **together.**
4. Water constitutes a fair part **of** human body.
5. A **group** of organisms of the same species.
6. Water **with** the highest salinity.
7. Amoeba is **an** organism.

V

1. Population level is **higher**/lower than biotic community in the organization hierarchy.
2. **Vaporisation** of water absorbs/releases energy.
3. Is the ratio of carbon **to** oxygen atoms in CO_2 is 2:1/1:2?
4. Is Kerosene miscible or immiscible **in** water?
5. Is solubility **of** copper sulphate higher or lower than that of common salt?
6. Is density of **ice** less or greater than that of water?

VI

1. Name the **chemical** which can cause brain damage in children.
2. Name the special behaviour which is shown **by** water.

ANSWERS

I

1. Preposition	2. Adjective
3. Verb	4. Preposition
5. Conjunction	6. Adjective
7. Noun	8. Pronoun
9. Verb	10. Preposition

II

1. Preposition	2. Adverb
3. Article (demonstrative adjective)	4. Preposition
5. Determiner (adjective)	

III

1. (Possessive) pronoun   **2.** Gerund (noun)

3. Modal (auxiliary verb)   **4.** Preposition

IV

1. Part participle (adjective)   **2.** During

3. Adverb   **4.** Preposition

5. (Collective) noun.   **6.** Preposition

7. Article (demonstrative adjective)

V

1. Adjective (comparative degree)   **2.** (abstract) noun

3. Preposition   **4.** Preposition

5. Preposition   **6.** (material) noun.

VI

1. Noun   **2.** Preposition.

ૐ૭

18. USE OF PREPOSITIONS
(LONG SENTENCES & PASSAGES)

Fill in the blanks (marked by ... (A) ... , ... (B) ... , ... (C)
... .) in the following sentences and short passages:—

1. The school lays stress ... (A) ... Spoken English. Realising the importance of music ... (B) ... life, students are made familiar ... (C) ... musical instruments.

2. Parent teacher meetings are held ... (A) ... monthly tests and terminal examinations. Parents are encouraged to contact teachers regularly ... (B) ... the betterment of their children. The school believes ... (C) ... Indian cultural and moral values. It has a secular outlook, hence moral values ... (D) ... all religions are taught ...   ... (E) ... the students ... (F) ... religious stories and ...   ... (G) ... performing religious activities like bhajans and shabad gyan etc.

3. I feel that field trips are useful ... (A) ... the educational point of view as traveling ... (B) ... different parts ... (C) ... the country imparts valuable practical education and teaches the students to live harmoniously and independently.

4. The objective ... (A) ... the fellowship was to train cardiac anesthetists on the latest trends and technologies ...   ... (B) ... better patient care ... (C) ... specialized training, quality cardiac care would further benefit the patients.

5. And although they do not pull you ... (A) ... the leash they can trip you over and even get trampled ... (B) ... a child. It is not easy to choose a pet and neither is it easy to keep one. Take your time. A life depends ... (C) ... your decision.

6. And if you have all the resources ... (A) ... keeping a gentle giant only then are they recommended as pets. There can be no greater pleasure than having a dog sit comfortably ... (B) ... your lap ... (C) ... a long hard day. Not only do small dogs cost less ... (D) ... maintenance, they are less dangerous ... (E) ... children. Whom would you prefer pulling ... (F) ... a leash, a Dane or a Pug?

7. "Measures like establishing a national institute ... (A) ... ... educating investors and amendment ... (B) ... definition ... (C) ... securities to include bonds ... (D) ... trading are positive," he said, adding, "a major positive impact would come as Foreign Institutional Investors (FIIs) can now give collateral ... (E) ... derivates. This would encourage derivatives trading."

8. "Now when they have been provided ... (A) ... all basic amenities ... (B) ... life, including drinking water and a most hygienic environment, the villagers can think ... (C) ... competing ... (D) ... the residents ... (E) ... the towns and cities," hoped Mr Decson.

9. "The FM has launched a number of proposals to sustain economic growth ... (A) ... increasing planned expenditure ... (B) ... education, health and infrastructure while maintaining a fine balance ... (C) ... having a prudent fiscal and revenue deficit." He said.

10. The decision to impose tax ... (A) ... withdrawals of Rs.10,000 per day ... (B) ... cash withdrawals evoked massive criticism. "It is a highly irrational decision. While details are yet to be seen, a transaction ... (C) ... Rs.10,000 ... (D) ... a businessman is a routine and if

the tax is ... (E) ... all segments business would be adversely affected," said Mr. Miglani.

11.   ... (A) ... Industry ... (B) ... the region it is certainly a positive Budget ... (C) ... relief and initiatives having come ... (D) ... the SSI segment and textile industry ... (E) ... the fact that the minister touched only textiles and sugar industry when it came ... (F) ... such major initiatives. He said the overhauling ... (G) ... income tax structure would mean that the assessees ... (H) ... income up to Rs. 2.5 lakh would benefit. However, FDI ... (I) ... mining and pensions is to be viewed ... (J) ... caution, he said.

12. Referring ... (A) ... the information received ... (B) ... the respective panches, they claimed that a majority ... (C) ... the beneficiaries had submitted correct particulars ... (D) ... their forms but the authorities ... (E) ... verifying the facts, chose to rely ... (F) ... information provided ... (G) ... unauthentic sources.

13. He said India was growing ... (A) ... a very fast pace ... (B) ... almost 8 per cent every year and the development which was taking place all ...(C)... the country, was a multidimensional process involving reorganization and reorientation ... (D) ... entire economic and social system. The public policies had a great impact ... (E) ... the pace and direction ... (F) ... the development ... (G) ... any economy.

14. However, the delivery system had to be very efficient and just for the same to happen, there was dire need ... (A) ... respect ... (B) ... human rights, right to information, accountability, justice and the public policy to be a mirror image ... (C) ... peoples' aspirations.

15. "Initiatives taken to help the industry meet global competition are welcome. The introduction ... (A) ... the

10 per cent capital subsidy scheme would go a long way ... (B) ... helping this industry. Reduction ... (C) ... Customs duty ... (D) ... 20 per cent ... (E) ... 10 per cent ... (F) ... textile machinery would help modernization he said.

16. He exclaimed that the association ... (A) ... the Canadian NRIs ... (B) ... their roots was wonderful and showed excellent results. Mr. Decson appreciated the excellence ... (C) ... the womenfolk ... (D) ... handicraft ... (E) ... watching an exhibition ... (F) ... the crafts arranged ... (G) ... the village panchayat on the occasion. He was presented some artifacts, which he said would be exhibited ... (H) ... the embassy.

17. It is mainly a breathing process where the rhythms are repeated ... (A) ... a cyclic fashion. He said, there existed a close link ... (B) ... the thoughts, emotions and the pattern ... (C) ... breathing and the "sudarshan kriya" harmonizes the three. He pointed out, the short breath reflects emotions like anger, excitement and fear, while the long and deep breath is reflective ... (D) ... a calm and peaceful mind. It simply happens to be a variation ... (E) ... the traditional pranayama practised ... (F) ... India ... (G) ... ages.

18. The French nationals were ... (A) ... the opinion that the cost ... (B) ... treatment ... (C) ... similar dental problems was not only five times more ... (D) ... their country, but the dental surgeons, like other medical experts, had a very long waiting list, particularly ... (E) ... cosmetic surgery. Moreover, the treatment that they had decided to get ... (F) ... India was not covered either ... (G) ... social security or the insurance companies. "... (H) ... one ... (I) ... my eye ailment, when I tried to get consultation ... (J) ... a specialist ... (K) ... October last year, I was told that the earliest appointment I could get will be ... (L) ... four months."

19. Dr. Bindra who has her own website said quite a few patients came ... (A) ... contact ... (B) ... her ... (C) ... internet while a sizeable number were referred ... (D) ... visiting NRIs ... (E) ... word ... (F) ... mouth. The winter months, particularly between December and Feburary suited them the most ... (G) ... the weather conditions and vacations ... (H) ... the schools and colleges. "... (I) ... these months, the number ... (J) ... patients coming ... (K) ... other countries goes up substantially," she said.

ANSWERS

(1)

(A) — on/upon	(B) — in	(C) — with

(2)

(A)— After	(B) — for	(C) — in
(D) — of	(E) — to	(F) — through
(G) — by		

(3)

(A)— from	(B) — to	(C) — of

(4)

(A)— behind	(B) — for	(C) — With

(5)

(A) — on	(B) — under	(C) — on

(6)

(A) — for	(B) — on	(C) — after
(D) — in	(E) — to	(F) — on

(7)

(A) — for	(B) — of	(C) — of
(D) — for	(E) — on	

(8)

(A) — with	(B) — of	(C) — of
(D) — with	(E) — of	

(9)

(A) — by	(B) — on	(C) — of

(10)

(A) — on	(B) — on	(C) — of
(D) — for	(E) — on	

(11)

(A) — For	(B) — in	(C) — with
(D) — for	(E) — despite/inspite of (F) — to	
(G) — of	(H) — with	(I) — in
(J) — with		

(12)

(A)— to	(B) — from	(C) — of
(D) — in	(E) — instead of	(F) — on
(G) — by		

(13)

(A)— At	(B) — of	(C) — round
(D) — of	(E) — on	(F) — of
(G) — of		

(14)

(A)— of	(B) — for	(C) — of

(15)

(A)— of	(B) — in	(C) — of
(D) —from	(E) — to	(F) — on

(16)

(A)— of   (B) — with   (C) — of

(D) — in   (E) — after   (F) — of

(G) — by   (H) — in

(17)

(A)— in   (B) — between   (C) — of

(D) — of   (E) — of   (F) — in

(G) — for

(18)

(A)— of   (B) — of   (C) — of

(D) — in   (E) — for   (F) — in

(G) — by   (H) — For   (I) — of

(J) — from   (K) — in   (L) — after

(19)

(A)— in   (B) — with   (C) — through

(D) — by   (E) — through   (F) — of

(G) — because of/owing to   (H) — in

(I) — During   (J) — of   (K) — from

☙

19. USE OF PREPOSITIONS

(RUNNING PASSAGES)

In the passages given below, prepositions have been omitted at most of the places. Such places are marked by a numbered blank space. Please fill in the appropriate preposition at each of the blank spaces:—

PASSAGE (1)

The Middle East has always been a source ... (1) ... crises and the present condition.... (2) ... the region is also quite delicate. This region being a major source ... (3) ... oil ... (4) ... the world, the present climate is a cause ... (5) ... concern ... (6) ... all oil importing countries including India.

Safety and security are ... (7) ... prime importance ... (8) ... the foreign tourists and the border conflict, communal tension ... (9) ... Gujarat and hostilities impact such tourist inflow.

PASSAGE (2)

Expenditure incurred ... (1) ... the first 5 years ... (2) ... crushing operations ... (3) ... plantation subsidy, transportation subsidy and sugar cane price paid ... (4) ... the cane growers ... (5) ... excess ... (6) ... support price fixed ... (7) ... the State Government is treated as cane development expenses and is written off ... (8) ... a period... (9) ... 5 years... (10) ... the year ... (11) ... which it is incurred.

PASSAGE (3)

... (1) ... our opinion and ... (2) ... the best of ... (3) ... our information and according ... (4) ... the explanations furnished ... (5) ... us, the said Balance Sheet and the Profit & Loss Account read together with the schedules and notes annexed therewith give the information as required ... (6) ... the Companies Act, 1956, ... (7) ... the manner so required and give a true and fair view.

PASSAGE (4)

We have obtained all the information and explanation, which to the best of our knowledge and belief were necessary ... (1) ... the purposes ... (2) ... our audit.

In our opinion, proper books ... (3) ... account as required ... (4) ... law have been kept ... (5) ... the company so far as appears ... (6) ... our examination ... (7) ... such books.

The Balance Sheet and the Profit & Loss Account dealt with ... (8) ... this report are ... (9) ... agreement ... (10) ... the books of account.

PASSAGE (5)

The company has not accepted any deposits ... (1) ... the public. Hence the provisions ... (2) ... section 58A ... (3) ... the Companies Act, 1956 and the Companies (Acceptance of Deposits) Rules, 1975, do not apply ... (4) ... this company.

The company has no by-products and has been ... (5) ... our opinion, maintaining reasonable records ... (6) ... the sale and disposal ... (7) ... realizable scrap.

In our opinion, the company has an internal audit system commensurate ... (8) ... the size and nature ... (9) ... its business

PASSAGE (6)

The Income tax authorities have made it mandatory ... (1) ... the person deducting income tax at source to quote the PAN/ GIR number in form 16A. We would request you to immediately furnish the PAN/GIR number to enable us to incorporate the same ... (2) ... Form 16A in future.

Members are requested to furnish particulars ... (3) ... their Bank, Name, MICR Code ... (4) ... Branch and Copy ... (5) ... cancelled Cheque leaf ... (6) ... their depository participant to facilitate remittance ... (7) ... future dividend ... (8) ... Electronic Clearing Service.

PASSAGE (7)

Members are requested to kindly notify the company ... (1) ... any change ... (2) ... their addresses so as to enable the company to address future communications ... (3) ... their addresses.

Members desiring any information as regards the accounts are requested to write ... (4) ... the company secretary at least a week ... (5) ... the meeting so as to enable the Management to reply ... (6) ... the Meeting.

Members are requested to kindly bring their copies ... (7) ... the annual Report ... (8) ... the Meeting.

PASSAGE (8)

The Hotel industry is a capital intensive one ... (1) ... high costs ... (2) ... real estate and construction and also heavy depreciation costs ... (3) ... the assets. ... (4) ... the growing stages the company has to bear heavy depreciation and interest costs as a result... (5) ... additions ... (6) ... existing capacities ... (7) ... the case ... (8) ... your company the burden ... (9) ... interest cost is practically non-existent, since there are no borrowings other than working capital. The relevant parameter ... (10) ... assessment ... (11) ... various units ... (12) ... the industry would therefore be EBITDA (Earnings ... (13) ... Interest, Tax Depreciation and Amortisation) or Operating Profit, rather than Profit ... (14) ... Tax, as the mix ... (15) ... assets would be different and would vary depending ... (16) ... whether the unit concerned is a fledgling or a fully grown one.

PASSAGE (9)

The political and economic environment ... (1) ... India is quite fluid and thus the hospitality industry continues to face a challenge. ... (2) ... the economic front, however, the GDP has grown ... (3) ... 6.4% which was primarily due to a recovery ... (4) ... the agricultural sector, thereby having no impact ... (5) ... the hospitality industry. The services sector on the whole seems to be recovering ... (6) ... the recent recession very slowly and, therefore, ... (7) ... the medium term, the industry's fortunes are likely to improve.

The industry is also facing risks ... (8) ... the volatile socio-political environment ... (9) ... the country resulting from the incidents of Gujarat and the concern ... (10) ... an Indo-Pak war.

PASSAGE (10)

Most ... (1) ... the economies ... (2) ... the world are coming out ... (3) ... their recent recession and are showing signs ... (4) ... growth. The US is displaying a rise ... (5) ... consumer spending which is likely to boost the confidence ... (6) ... European and Asian economies. Many ... (7) ... the Asian economies, including India are already placed as stable economies. Technological spends are likely to increase, which could improve the prospects ... (8) ... the service industry. This should augur well ... (9) ... the hotel industry also, as a chunk ... (10) ... our business comes ... (11) ... the service industry.

PASSAGE (11)

India has emerged as a strong performer ... (1) ... the world scenario ... (2) ... the last financial year. The Budget... (3) ... (year) has focussed ... (4) ... the continuation ... (5) ... reforms, as a result ... (6) ... which liberalization is anticipated to gain further momentum.

The stability ... (7) ... the Government ... (8) ... the Centre has boosted the confidence ... (9) ... the business community ... (10)

... the country. The effect ... (11) ... the reforms and the increasing confidence can be evidenced ... (12) ... the increase ... (13) ... Foreign Direct Investment and the Foreign Exchange Reserves ... (14) ... the country. This trend ... (15) ... reforms and liberalization is expected to continue.

PASSAGE (12)

Your company has an adequate system ... (1) ... internal control, which ensures that all transactions are duly authorised and recorded. The system also prevents its assets ... (2) ... loss ... (3) ... wastage and unauthorized use and removal.

The adequacy and effectiveness ... (4) ... internal controls are monitored regularly ... (5) ... the Internal Auditors and remedial measures are adopted, where necessary. Internal Audit ... (6) ... the year initially covered the compliance check ... (7) ... the previous years recommendations and then went ... (8) ... a comprehensive and exhaustive review ... (9) ... certain key control areas. The Internal Auditors have confirmed that the existing control systems have improved further.

Your company's statutory auditors have assessed the internal control procedures and the functioning ... (10) ... the internal auditors and have confirmed the adequacy ... (11) ... the same ... (12) ... their report.

PASSAGE (13)

We conducted our audit ... (1) ... auditing standards generally accepted ... (2) ... India. Those standards require that we plan and perform the audit to obtain reasonable assurance ... (3) ... whether the financial statements are free ... (4) ... material misstatement. An audit includes examining ... (5) ... a test basis, evidence supporting the amounts and disclosures ... (6) ... the financial statements. An Audit also includes assessing the accounting principles used and significant estimates made ...

(7) ... management, as well as evaluating the overall financial statements presentation. We believe that our audit provides a reasonable basis ... (8) ... our opinion.

PASSAGE (14)

The stocks ... (1) ... stores and operating supplies, food and beverages have been physically verified ... (2) ... the year ... (3) ... the management. ... (4) ... our opinion, the frequency ... (5) ... the verification is reasonable.

The procedures ... (6) ... physical verification ... (7) ... stocks followed ... (8) ... the management are reasonable and adequate ... (9) ... relation ... (10) ... the size ... (11) ... the company and the nature ... (12) ... its business.

The discrepances noticed ... (13) ... verification... (14) ... the physical stocks and the book records were not material.

... (15) ... the basis ... (16) ... our examination... (17) ... stock records, we are ... (18) ... the opinion that the valuation ... (19) ... stocks is fair and proper ... (20) ... the normally accepted accounting principles and is ... (21) ... the same basis as ... (22) ... the preceding year.

PASSAGE (15)

The company has not given any loans ... (1) ... companies, firms and other parties listed ... (2) ... the registers maintained ... (3) ... section 301 or ... (4) ... Companies ... (5) ... the same management ... (6) ... the meaning ... (7) ... section 370 (1B) ... (8) ... the Companies Act, 1956. ... (9) ... respect... (10) ...advances ... (11) ... employees... (12) ... the company the said employees have been repaying the loans, which are non-interest bearing.

In our opinion and... (13) ... the information and explanations given ... (14) ... us there are adequate internal control procedures commensurate... (15) ... the size... (16) ... the company and the nature... (17) ... its business ... (18) ... regard... (19) ... purchases... (20) ... the stores and operating supplies, Food and Beverage,

Plant & Machinery Equipment, other assets and ... (21) ... the sale... (22) ... goods.

PASSAGE (16)

... (1) ...to the information and explanations given... (2) ... us, no personal expenses... (3) ... employees or directors have been charged... (4) ... revenue account other than those payable... (5) ... contractual obligations or... (6) ... generally accepted business practice.

The provisions... (7) ... the Sick Industrial Companies (Special Provisions) Act, 1985 are not applicable... (8) ... this company. ... (9) ... our opinion the company has a reasonable system ... (10) ... recording receipts issues and consumption... (11) ... material and stores commensurate ... (12) ... its size and nature ... (13) ... its business.

Clause 4(B)(iii)... (14) ... the above order is not applicable ... (15) ... this company. ... (16) ... our opinion there is a reasonable system ... (17) ... authorization ... (18) ... proper levels and adequate system... (19) ... internal control commensurate ... (20) ... the size ... (21) ... the company and nature ... (22) ... its business... (23) ... issue and allocation ... (24) ... stores.

ANSWERS-1

1. of	**2.** in	**3.** of	**4.** for
5. for	**6.** for	**7.** of	**8.** to
9. in			

ANSWERS-2

1. during	**2.** of	**3.** towards	**4.** to
5. in	**6.** of		

(**Note:** In excess of itself is a phrase preposition).

7. by	**8.** over	**9.** of	**10.** from
11. in			

ANSWERS-3

1. In **2.** to **3.** of **4.** to

(**Note :** 'to the best of' and 'according to' in themselves are phrase preposition)

5. to **6.** by **7.** in

ANSWERS-4

1. for **2.** of **3.** of **4.** by

5. by **6.** from **7.** of **8.** by

9. in **10.** with

(**Note:** 'for the purposes of' and 'in agreement with' are themselves phrase prepositions.)

ANSWERS-5

1. from **2.** of **3.** of **4.** to

5. in **6.** for **7.** of **8.** with

9. of

ANSWERS-6

1. for **2.** in **3.** of **4.** of

5. of **6.** to **7.** of **8.** by

ANSWERS-7

1. of **2.** in **3.** to **4.** to

5. before **6.** at **7.** of **8.** to

ANSWERS-8

1. with **2.** of **3.** on **4.** In

5. of **6.** to **7.** In **8.** of

(**Note :** 'In case of' is a phrase preposition)

9. of **10.** for **11.** of **12.** in

13. before **14.** after **15.** of **16.** upon

ANSWERS-9

1. in	**2.** on	**3.** by	**4.** in
5. on	**6.** from	**7.** in	**8.** from
9. in	**10.** about		

ANSWERS-10

1. of	**2.** of	**3.** of	**4.** of
5. in	**6.** of	**7.** of	**8.** for
9. for	**10.** of	**11.** from	

ANSWERS-11

1. in	**2.** during	**3.** for	**4.** on
5. of	**6.** of	**7.** of	**8.** at
9. of	**10.** in	**11.** of	**12.** by
13. in	**14.** of	**15.** of	

ANSWERS-12

1. of	**2.** against	**3.** from	**4.** of
5. by	**6.** during	**7.** of	**8.** into
9. of	**10.** of	**11.** of	**12.** in

ANSWERS-13

1. in accordance with	**2.** in	**3.** about	
4. of	**5.** on	**6.** in	**7.** by
8. for			

ANSWERS-14

1. of	**2.** during	**3.** by	**4.** In
5. of	**6.** of	**7.** of	**8.** by
9. in	**10.** to	**11.** of	**12.** of
13. on	**14.** between	**15.** On	**16.** of

17. of   **18.** of   **19.** of

20. in accordance with   **21.** on   **22.** in

(**Note :** 'In relation to' and 'on the basis of' are phrase preposition)

ANSWERS-15

1. to   **2.** in   **3.** under   **4.** to

5. under   **6.** within   **7.** of   **8.** of

9. In   **10.** of   **11.** to   **12.** of

13. according to   **14.** to   **15.** with   **16.** of

17. of   **18.** with   **19.** to   **20.** of

21. for   **22.** of

(**Note :** "within the meaning of", "in respect of" and " with reagard to" are phrase prepositions.")

ANSWERS-16

1. According to   **2.** to   **3.** of   **4.** to

5. under   **6.** in accordance with   **7.** of

8. to   **9.** In   **10.** of   **11.** of

12. with   **13.** of   **14.** of   **15.** to

16. In   **17.** of   **18.** at   **19.** of

20. with   **21.** of   **22.** of   **23.** on

24. of

ଓ ଓ

20. CHOOSING THE RIGHT ALTERNATIVE—I

Choose the right alternative from the given options:

1. We must abide __________ the laws of our country.
   a. by   b. to
2. There is enough water__________ this jug for you and me.
   a. within   b. in
3. Let us hope__________ the best.
   a. for   b. to
4. Books are said to be the best treasure __________ man's heritage.
   a. of   b. in
5. Divide this apple__________ two boys.
   a. among   b. between
6. Whom are you waiting__________?
   a. at   b. for
7. I agree__________ you.
   a. with   b. to
8. Why are you angry __________him?
   a. at   b. with
9. I agreed __________ his proposal.
   a. with   b. to
10. He was born __________ Delhi.
    a. in   b. at

11. We are all answerable __________ God for our deeds.

    a. at   b. to

12. Can you climb __________ a tree?

    a. to   b. up

13. What is __________ this bag?

    a. inside   b. from

14. Do not prevent me __________ going there.

    a. from   b. to

15. He insisted __________ accompanying me.

    a. at   b. on

16. You must look __________ your ailing mother.

    a. after   b. on

17. Open your books __________ page ten.

    a. at   b. on

18. There is a temple __________ the river.

    a. besides   b. beside

19. Look __________ the blackboard.

    a. at   b. on

20. It is no use crying __________ spilt milk.

    a. at   b. over

21. Has the train met __________ an accident?

    a. with   b. at

22. He is blind __________ one eye.

    a. of   b. off

23. She has come __________ age.

    a. of   b. off

24. __________ which building is your office housed?

    a. At   b. In

25. What are you looking __________ here?
a. against   b. for

26. Please bear __________ us.
a. with   b. upon

27. __________ whom were you defeated?
a. By   b. With

28. The hunter killed the lion __________ a gun.
a. by   b. with

29. The police is looking __________ this matter.
a. at   b. into

30. The trader was killed __________ the robbers.
a. by   b. over

31. We'll talk __________ a cup of tea.
a. over   b. with

32. He is not on speaking terms __________ me.
a. to   b. with

33. Wait here __________ 5 o' clock.
a. till   b. before

34. We'll reach home __________ sunset.
a. through   b. before

35. Many a blessing has been bestowed by God __________ mankind.
a. in   b. upon

36. He is hoping __________ hope.
a. for   b. against

37. We should not quarrel __________ anybody.
a. with   b. for

38. He praised you __________ your courage.
a. for   b. over

39. Our teacher doesn't teach the students _______ their head.

    a. into   b. above

40. Be true _______ yourself.

    a. to   b. with

41. Do good _______ others.

    a. with   b. to

42. She burst _______ tears.

    a. into   b. out

43. Think _______ this matter.

    a. at   b. over

44. Set your house _______ order.

    a. at   b. in

45. At last, I brought him over _______ my views.

    a. at   b. to

46. I do not care a fig _______ him.

    a. for   b. at

47. Excess of work told _______ his health.

    a. upon   b. at

48. Yesterday India launched another Sputnik _______ space.

    a. for   b. into

49. Fishes swim _______ water.

    a. in   b. over

50. We sit _______ fire in the evening.

    a. by   b. with

51. Do not play _______ fire.

    a. with   b. on

52. He began to tremble _______ fear.

a. for   b. with

53. Spread this cloth __________ the table.

a. at   b. over

54. Is he still fiddling __________ this idea?

a. with   b. at

55. Who is there __________ the room?

a. in   b. into

56. Please put the book __________ the table.

a. upon   b. on

57. He went __________ the road.

a. over   b. across

58. The cat jumped __________ the table.

a. upon   b. on

59. The frog jumped __________ the well.

a. into   b. in

60. This table is made __________ wood.

a. with   b. of

61. They were made __________ each other.

a. for   b. through

62. How can we get __________ this difficult situation ?

a. over   b. on

63. It is raining __________ the mountains.

a. over   b. in

64. Your words are __________ the mark.

a. off   b. of

65. Let's face the situation __________ courage.

a. with   b. through

66. It is very hot __________ the house.

    a. out of   b. outside

67. We went there _________ train.

    a. by   b. through

68. I came _________ contact with him by chance.

    a. at   b. into

69. He told me these facts _________ the condition of anonymity.

    a. for   b. on

70. You must stick _________ your view point.

    a. at   b. to

71. From Srinagar we proceeded _________ Badrinath.

    a. to   b. on

72. The sun sets _________ the west.

    a. at   b. in

73. Has she complained _________ you?

    a. against   b. for

74. Have you applied _________ this post?

    a. to   b. for

75. I could not comply _________ his request.

    a. with   b. to

76. Please think _________ this matter.

    a. over   b. at

77. I'll cut him _________ size.

    a. on   b. to

78. Let this lesson be learnt _________ all.

    a. by   b. for

79. It is a lesson _________ you.

    a. by   b. for

80. She is just __________ her mother.

a. as   b. like

81. We had to fight __________ heavy odds.

a. against   b. over

82. I took pity __________ the beggar.

a. on   b. for

83. I sympathised __________ him.

a. with   b. at

84. He is secular __________ his outlook.

a. at   b. in

85. He objected __________ my remarks.

a. to   b. for

86. We should not tamper __________ official records.

a. with   b. for

87. Most of the people run __________ money.

a. after   b. with

88. The robbers ran away __________ the booty.

a. for   b. with

89. The robbers did away __________ the trader.

a. with   b. to

90. You must act __________ your parents' advice.

a. for   b. upon

91. Can I bank __________ your help?

a. at   b. on

92. Terrorism is certainly a cause __________ concern.

a. for   b. of

93. He has turned __________ a new leaf of life.

a. over   b. out

94. He dwelt __________ the matter at great length.

a. out   b. on

95. I invited him __________ my brother's marriage.

a. to   b. for

96. I congratulate you __________ your success in the examination.

a. on   b. in

97. Oranges are sold __________ the dozen.

a. with   b. by

98. What is the rate of these oranges __________ dozen?

a. per   b. at

99. It is all __________ the bargain.

a. into   b. for

100. When is the party going to make the final assault __________ the summit?

a. on   b. over

101. He is __________ head and ears in debt.

a. beside   b. over

102. When will the __________ train come?

a. down   b. below

103. Your letter is replete __________ errors.

a. with   b. for

104. Why are you annoyed __________ him ?

a. at   b. with

105. What is contained __________ this vessel?

a. in   b. by

106. I am greatly surprised __________ your behaviour.

a. at   b. for

107. Has the culprit been brought __________ book?

    a. over   b. to

108. The cow feeds __________ grass.

    a. with   b. on

109. Caustic soda eats __________ aluminium.

    a. into   b. at

110. I had only a bite __________ bread in the morning.

    a. for   b. of

111. Why are you beating __________ the bush?

    a. about   b. on

112. All of us are the children __________ God.

    a. of   b. through

113. He is not a man to be relied __________.

    a. at   b. on

114. You need not weep __________ the past.

    a. over   b. at

115. The sky is overcast __________ dark clouds.

    a. with   b. for

116. He swore __________ God to prove his innocence.

    a. at   b. by

117. There are hardly any who can row __________ the current.

    a. against   b. with

118. The servant proved true __________ his salt.

    a. to   b. for

119. I had an inkling __________ the things to come.

    a. for   b. of

120. He brought a slur __________ the fair face of his family.

    a. at   b. on

121. I'll stand __________ you at all costs.

    a. for   b. by

122. I've called __________ his explanation.

    a. out   b. for

123. Do not hanker __________ riches.

    a. at   b. after

124. Don't be crazy __________ new fashions.

    a. about   b. at

125. Call __________ the doctor.

    a. on   b. in

126. Why have you come __________ the room?

    a. into   b. in

127. She was born __________ 5 May.

    a. on   b. in

128. He was born __________ rich parents.

    a. of   b. from

129. He hails __________ Bangladesh.

    a. from   b. to

130. This matter calls __________ immediate attention.

    a. to   b. for

131. She broke down __________ the middle of her speech.

    a. into   b. in

132. He deals __________ sugar.

    a. into   b. in

133. She is __________ the beck and call of her parents.

    a. on   b. at

134. He has grown up __________ a fine young man.

    a. into   b. over

135. I'm in agreement __________ you in this matter.

    a. with   b. to

136. Birds __________ a feather flock together.

    a. with   b. of

137. I was greatly impressed __________ his simple manners.

    a. by   b. for

138. Are you annoyed __________ his conduct?

    a. at   b. for

139. We should put a bid __________ the matter.

    a. on   b. to

140. The train arrived __________ the station on time.

    a. on   b. at

141. Your remarks are an insult __________ the fair name of your family.

    a. on   b. to

142. Are you equipped __________ all kinds of necessary item?

    a. with   b. at

143. I'm ready __________ the show.

    a. at   b. for

144. Your action bears testimony __________ your honesty of purpose.

    a. to   b. at

145. Are you afraid __________ the dog?

    a. of   b. at

146. The boss has dispensed __________ the services of the lazy worker.

    a. with   b. to

147. They never fail who fail __________ a noble cause.

    a. to   b. in

148. Are things going on __________ the plan?

a. according to b. along

149. He could not finish the work in time __________ ill health.

a. for the sake of   b. because of

150. I gave a slap __________ his face.

a. through   b. across

151. The news spread __________ wild fire.

a. against   b. like

152. The news spread all __________ the world.

a. in   b. over

153. He abstains __________ meat.

a. from   b. to

154. We should refrain __________ telling lies.

a. from   b. at

155. I have put him __________ a spot (colloq).

a. at   b. in

156. I can't live __________ you.

a. for   b. without

157. We must keep such people __________ bay.

a. at   b. to

158. I do not care __________ him.

a. to   b. for

159. He is a wolf __________ sheep's clothing.

a. of   b. in

160. She is shivering __________ cold.

a. with   b. for

161. He dived __________ the pond.

a. in   b. into

162. The dog jumped __________ the wall.

a. over   b. through

163. I at once saw __________ his game.

a. through   b. at

164. I'll help you __________ thick and thin.

a. in   b. through

165. He's a patriot __________ the bone.

a. at   b. to

166. The poor fellow died __________ inches.

a. by   b. in

167. What do we get when we divide ten __________ two?

a. into   b. by

168. Everything will be done __________ your wishes.

a. to   b. in accordance with

169. There is always a calm __________ the storm.

a. after   b. before

170. What makes you so indifferent __________ your friends?

a. to   b. with

171. There was none __________ wept.

a. that   b. but

172. None __________ him can solve this sum.

a. except   b. without

173. Please look __________ this matter.

a. in   b. into

174. He showed hesitation __________ joining the new party.

a. at   b. in

175. Do not put off __________ tomorrow what you can do today.

a. upto   b. till

176. Let us wait __________ him.

a. for   b. with

177. He knows nothing __________ good manners.

a. about   b. over

178. His conduct is __________ suspicion.

a. for   b. above

179. She is __________ fifty years old.

a. over   b. on

180. I saw him wandering __________ the road.

a. along   b. with

181. He is __________ the wrong side of forty.

a. on   b. in

182. You are __________ the wrong.

a. in   b. over

183. There is a bridge __________ the river.

a. at   b. across

184. To do this is not __________ my powers.

a. within   b. of

185. How much electricity do you consume __________ month?

a. each   b. per

186. Ashoka reigned __________ a vast empire.

a. over   b. on

187. We'll reach our destination __________ evening.

a. at   b. by

188. The train will reach Delhi __________ 5 o'clock.

a. on   b. after

189. He had to join the army __________ his will.

a. against   b. due to

190. There is often a silver lining __________ the dark cloud.

a. in   b. on

191. It has been raining __________ morning.

a. for   b. since

192. The gardener has been watering the plants __________ two hours.

a. for   b. since

193. This pen differs __________ that.

a. to   b. from

194. It is five __________ ten now.

a. over   b. past

195. Honesty pays __________ the long run.

a. in   b. at

196. Don't feel perturbed __________ this trifling matter.

a. over   b. from

197. He is wearing a ring __________ his finger.

a. on   b. round

198. Please tell me something __________ ghosts.

a. about   b. for

199. __________ which bookseller did you purchase this book?

a. Of   b. From

200. You are only labouring __________ a misunderstanding.

a. under   b. over

201. __________ which state does he belong?

a. From   b. To

202. __________ which address did you send the letter?

a. To   b. At

203. This college is affiliated __________ the Andhra University.

    a. at   b. to

204. The swimmer kept his head __________ the water.

    a. above   b. on

205. Please don't go __________ the hall.

    a. from   b. inside

206. Why did the train halt __________ the station?

    a. outside   b. under

207. Nobody knows what is there __________ the sky.

    a. beyond   b. at

208. Have you any other pen __________ this one?

    a. apart   b. besides

209. Please sit __________ me.

    a. beside   b. besides

210. Beware __________ pickpockets.

    a. of   b. off

ANSWERS

1	2	3	4	5	6	7	8	9	10
a	b	a	a	b	b	a	b	b	a
11	**12**	**13**	**14**	**15**	**16**	**17**	**18**	**19**	**20**
b	b	a	a	b	a	a	b	a	b
21	**22**	**23**	**24**	**25**	**26**	**27**	**28**	**29**	**30**
a	a	a	a	b	a	a	b	a	a
31	**32**	**33**	**34**	**35**	**36**	**37**	**38**	**39**	**40**
a	b	a	b	b	b	a	a	b	a
41	**42**	**43**	**44**	**45**	**46**	**47**	**48**	**49**	**50**
b	a	b	b	b	a	a	b	a	a
51	**52**	**53**	**54**	**55**	**56**	**57**	**58**	**59**	**60**
a	b	b	a	a	b	b	a	a	b
61	**62**	**63**	**64**	**65**	**66**	**67**	**68**	**69**	**70**
a	a	a	a	a	b	a	b	b	b

71	**72**	**73**	**74**	**75**	**76**	**77**	**78**	**79**	**80**
a	b	a	b	a	a	b	a	b	b
81	**82**	**83**	**84**	**85**	**86**	**87**	**88**	**89**	**90**
a	a	a	b	a	a	a	b	a	b
91	**92**	**93**	**94**	**95**	**96**	**97**	**98**	**99**	**100**
b	b	a	b	a	a	b	a	a	a
101	**102**	**103**	**104**	**105**	**106**	**107**	**108**	**109**	**110**
b	a	a	b	a	a	b	b	a	b
111	**112**	**113**	**114**	**115**	**116**	**117**	**118**	**119**	**120**
a	a	b	a	a	b	a	a	b	b
121	**122**	**123**	**124**	**125**	**126**	**127**	**128**	**129**	**130**
b	b	b	a	b	a	a	a	a	b
131	**132**	**133**	**134**	**135**	**136**	**137**	**138**	**139**	**140**
b	b	b	a	a	b	a	a	a	b
141	**142**	**143**	**144**	**145**	**146**	**147**	**148**	**149**	**150**
b	a	b	a	a	a	b	a	b	b
151	**152**	**153**	**154**	**155**	**156**	**157**	**158**	**159**	**160**
b	b	a	a	b	b	a	b	b	a
161	**162**	**163**	**164**	**165**	**166**	**167**	**168**	**169**	**170**
b	a	a	b	b	a	b	b	b	a
171	**172**	**173**	**174**	**175**	**176**	**177**	**178**	**179**	**180**
a	a	b	b	b	a	a	b	a	a
181	**182**	**183**	**184**	**185**	**186**	**187**	**188**	**189**	**190**
a	a	b	a	b	a	b	b	a	a
191	**192**	**193**	**194**	**195**	**196**	**197**	**198**	**199**	**200**
b	a	b	b	a	a	a	a	b	a
201	**202**	**203**	**204**	**205**	**206**	**207**	**208**	**209**	**210**
b	a	b	a	b	a	a	b	a	a

☙❧

21. CHOOSING THE RIGHT ALTERNATIVE—II

In each of the following sentences, there are two blanks. Below each sentence four alternatives are given. You have to choose the right alternatives for blanks from those given alternatives:

1. Let us wait _________ him _________ 5 o' clock.

   a. to   b. for   c. on   d. till

2. It is not good _________ you to lose your temper _________ this ordinary matter.

   a. for   b. from   c. over   d. of

3. The river ran _________ the valley _________ a charming way.

   a. at   b. through   c. in   d. of

4. Can you bring _________ memory those happy days when we bathed _________ the river so happily?

   a. on   b. for   c. in   d. to

5. You should not have beaten the dog _________ a stick even if it had barked _________ you.

   a. at   b. with   c. across   d. on

6. Please sit close _________ me so that we can exchange our views _________ this matter.

   a. about   b. at   c. to   d. for

7. _________ all that has happened, let us hope _________ the best.

   a. because of   b. for   c. in spite of   d. into

8. She began to look ________ the plants ________ the grassy path.

    a. at   b. along   c. into   d. for

9. You should not express your views ________ this document until you have looked ________ it.

    a. about   b. for   c. through   d. in

10. Let us all do our best to do away ________ poverty because it is known ________ all that it is a great curse.

    a. with   b. for   c. to   d. at

11. I am surprised ________ your capacity ________ doing so much work.

    a. with   b. at   c. for   d. to

12. I made adequate arrangements ________ the stay of guests and ordered that they should be provided ________ all the eatables they demanded.

    a. for   b. to   c. with   d. in

13. I'll stand ________ you ________ thick and thin.

    a. through   b. in   c. by   d. with

14. The soldiers put ________ the resistance ________ a long time.

    a. for   b. up   c. out of   d. within

15. We must live ________ our means if we want to make real progress ________ life.

    a. out of   b. beyond   c. in   d. within

16. Since I have been divested ________ many of my powers, it is now ________ my powers to accede to your request.

    a. of   b. in   c. beyond   d. through

17. Having entered the services ________ the backdoor, he only poses to be a man ________ great merit.

    a. through   b. in   c. of   d. off

18. We should not bother excessively ________ difficulties as we are bound to be confronted ________ them at every step in life.

    a. on   b. about   c. with   d. at

19. I took him ________ a friend but he turned out to be an enemy ________ the worst kind.

    a. for   b. of   c. with   d. on

20. I invited him ________ tea and served him delicacies ________ all kinds.

    a. at   b. to   c. of   d. with

21. We can learn a lot ________ books written ________ great man.

    a. in   b. by   c. from   d. to

22. The thing that is very particular ________ him is that he never compromises ________ principles.

    a. about   b. at   c. for   d. with

23. He is devoid ________ sense and nothing spectacular can be expected ________ him.

    a. of   b. of   c. in   d. at

24. It is often said ________ the wise people that there is always sufficient room ________ the top.

    a. in   b. over   c. at   d. by

25. It is rarely that progress is made ________ leap and bounds. It is often the result ________ long, hard efforts.

    a. by   b. in   c. of   d. with

26. Be careful ________ the pennies and the pounds will take care ________ themselves.

    a. of   b. about   c. at   d. for

27. Try to think deeply ________ what anybody says; at is simply ridiculous to make light ________ others' words.

    a. at   b. over   c. of   d. on

28. He is good __________ history but he is weak __________ geography.

    a. in   b. over   c. at   d. with

29. We buy oranges __________ the hundred but we sell them __________ small numbers.

    a. in   b. with   c. by   d. at

30. He lived __________ India __________ five years.

    a. in   b. for   c. till   d. over

31. Being tired __________ the life here, he has left this place __________ good.

    a. to   b. for   c. of   d. with

32. Being contented __________ his lot, he never runs __________ money.

    a. with   b. of   c. after   d. in

33. When the policeman started running __________ the thief, the latter ran __________ his life.

    a. for   b. after   c. over   d. in

34. Please ponder __________ what he has said __________ rushing to arrive at any conclusion.

    a. for   b. before   c. over   d. on

35. Things have come to such a pass that it is becoming increasingly difficult __________ a common man to keep the wolf __________ the door.

    a. with   b. for   c. outside   d. from

36. We should not look down __________ others nor find fault __________ anybody.

    a. upon   b. with   c. over   d. to

37. It is only a matter __________ minutes when the stars appear __________ the sky.

    a. for   b. in   c. of   d. at

38. Always look _________ the bright side _________ things.

a. outside   b. within   c. of   d. at

39. Never tell anybody what you have _________ mind until your friendship _________ him is well-established.

a. in   b. about   c. with   d. at

40. When one is engrossed _________ past memories, one has the tendency to brood _________ trivial happenings.

a. at   b. in   c. with   d. over

41. Never think ill _________ others nor gloss _________ your own faults.

a. at   b. over   c. of   d. with

42. It depends _________ an individual to choose good _________ bad.

a. upon/on   b. from   c. for   d. in

43. Both these sticks look _________ flutes. You are to guess the real one _________ these.

a. out of   b. like   c. past   d. upon

44. Much water has flowed _________ the Ganga _________ India declared its policy of peaceful co-existence with its neighbours.

a. since   b. before   c. down   d. on

45. I could make neither head nor tail _________ what he said _________ the influence of liquor.

a. over   b. under   c. at   d. of

46. The two trains which were running _________ a very high speed collided _________ each other at a flag-station.

a. at   b. with   c. from   d. in

47. The two buses which were coming _________ opposite directions collided and gave a powerful jolt _________ the passengers.

a. with   b. from   c. to   d. toward

48. The lion was advancing slowly __________ the dear __________ the dark.

    a. in   b. towards   c. for   d. with

49. The making __________ a nation is a great task and all the citizens should participate __________ this noble venture.

    a. of   b. in   c. out   d. at

50. There is always a great demand __________ qualitative goods, but this simple fact is __________ the understanding of some unscrupulous manufacturers.

    a. with   b. for   c. beyond   d.with

51. __________ democracy aspirations __________ the common people cannot be ignored.

    a. of   b. in   c. with   d. for

52. Those who stand too much __________ceremonies should not play __________ others' crude ways of living.

    a. on   b. of   c. down   d. over

53. He was put __________ great hardships but he bore __________ all this.

    a. over   b. through   c. at   d. with

54. Our ancient heritage is something most precious __________ us and we cannot part __________ it at any cost.

    a. to   b. with   c. for   d. from

55. It may be easy to part company __________ a common friend but it is always painful to part __________ your best friend.

    a. from   b. to   c. with   d. for

56. I'm __________ no mood to lay bear my heart to you if you are not ready to listen __________ me most attentively.

    a. on   b. in   c. to   d. for

57. I continued my efforts _________ a very subtle manner and succeeded in winning _________ her heart.

    a. in   b. over   c. with   d. at

58. The two friends fell out _________ each other _________ a trifle.

    a. over   b. for   c. with   d. till

59. You will have to walk _________ a long distance _________ reaching the port.

    a. on   b. up   c. over   d. before

60. Everybody is wise _________ the accident but hardly anybody is wise _________ the accident.

    a. after   b. with   c. at   d. before

61. The demonstrators were chanting _________ a loud voice, "Down _________ the tyrant"!

    a. in   b. with   c. at   d. to

62. All my efforts _________ bringing about a compromise _________ the two parties failed.

    a. about   b. for   c. between   d. at

63. If you want to maintain your peace _________ mind, I'd advise you to patch up _________ him.

    a. of   b. to   c. with   d. for

64. He seems to be in _________ some trouble as these days he is giving airs _________ his naughty views about others.

    a. at   b. to   c. for   d. with

65. _________ making a lot of mistakes, at last wisdom dawned _________ him.

    a. after   b. without   c. on   d. at

66. It is, indeed, a wonder _________ the carpenter's skill that of these two tables it is difficult to distinguish one _________ the other.

    a. at   b. from   c. of   d. in

67. He is suffering __________ colour blindness and as such cannot distinguish __________ green and blue.

    a. at   b. from   c. among   d. between

68. __________ all the books that I have read this one has appealed __________ me the most.

    a. among   b. in   c. to   d. from

69. Employees who were found absent __________ duty were dismissed and those who were present were given offers __________ promotion.

    a. for   b. of   c. from   d. to

70. Avenues __________ progress are almost non-existent __________ this part of the country.

    a. to   b. in   c. on   d. at

71. Life is always miserable __________ those who cannot cope __________ its rigours.

    a. with   b. at   c. in   d. for

72. From the outside the house seemed to be made __________ some cheap material but __________ it I found the floor and walls covered with slabs of marble.

    a. of   b. inside   c. of   d. from

73. __________ his hungry looks I judged that he was a man __________ jealousy in his mind.

    a. with   b. in   c. from   d. for

74. Those who give way __________ despair have never pondered __________ the gifts which life has given them.

    a. to   b. over   c. at   d. for

75. Payment of wages __________ the workers was withheld by the management with a view to pressurizing them to call __________ the strike.

    a. on   b. to   c. off   d. at

76. This new model __________ machine is an improvement __________ the previous one.

    a. of   b. at   c. over   d. in

77. Much can be said __________ and __________ the proposal.

    a. with   b. for   c. between   d. against

78. He follows the policy of hunting __________ the hunter and running __________ the hare.

    a. with   b. with   c. to   d. on

79. Do not poke your nose __________ others' affairs as such activities can bring discredit __________ your reputation.

    a. into   b. for   c. to   d. against

80. All the evidence points __________ your involvement __________ the affair.

    a. at   b. in   c. to   d. with

81. Apart __________ being insulted, he was subjected __________ great cruelties.

    a. from   b. with   c. at   d. to

82. "__________ the frying pan __________ the fire" is a common saying.

    a. of   b. from   c. at   d. into

83. __________ all his faults, I have a great regard __________ him in my heart.

    a. for   b. to   c. with   d. in

84. __________ working hard he could not get __________ the examination.

    a. because of   b. in spite of   c. through   d. at

85. As soon as the government's policy __________ new taxes was announced, there were loud protests __________ the country.

    a. throughout   b. over   c. of   d. on

86. He played ducks and drakes __________ his father's wealth and is now __________ head and ears in debt.

 a. with   b. in   c. over   d. at

87. It is a quotation __________ Pope's "Essay on Man" that "Proper study __________ mankind is man".

 a. from   b. over   c. of   d. at

88. We may deny comfort __________ ourselves but we should not deprive others __________ it.

 a. of   b. with   c. to   d. on

89. He was booked __________ the police __________ having embezzled __________ public funds.

 a. with   b. on   c. by   d. for

90. The ship struck __________ the rocks and broke __________ pieces.

 a. over   b. with   c. into   d. against

91. The main reason __________ his being disliked by the people is that his appearance is __________ him.

 a. with   b. on   c. against   d. for

92. The children should not be allowed __________ the mothers to move out of the house__________ dark.

 a. by   b. after   c. over   d. at

93. I saw two gypsies __________ a distance as I was walking __________ the lane.

 a. down   b. from   c. outside   d. over

94. He made a gesture __________ me to sit __________ him.

 a. beside   b. for   c. in   d. to

95. The workers gathered __________ the gate of the mill to raise their voice __________ the new policy of the management.

 a. near   b. with   c. against   d. to

96. He is __________ fifty but already he is hard __________ hearing.

    a. in   b. below   c. of   d. with

97. Those who have no regard __________ their elders can never get success __________ life.

    a. of   b. in   c. for   d. to

98. He is bent __________ mischief. As such you must not turn a blind eye __________ his activities.

    a. over   b. on   c. with   d. to

99. I cannot rely __________ him as he is habituated __________ telling lies.

    a. at   b. with   c. to   d. on

100. I was glad to find that the feeling __________ the meeting was __________ the proposal.

    a. for   b. of   c. over   d. under

101. __________ what place does the diversification __________ the stream take place?

    a. to   b. at   c. of   d. in

102. The division __________ his field and mine is marked __________ a thick hedge.

    a. for   b. by   c. between   d. among

103. Being afraid __________ the prowling hyena, we had to hide __________ the bushes in the forest.

    a. for   b. of   c. among   d. between

104. Two neighbouring countries must always live __________ amity __________ each other.

    a. for   b. with   c. in   d. over

105. He is a man __________ evil nature and is not amenable __________ reason.

    a. of   b. towards   c. to   d. for

106. Don't worry, there's ample room _________ all of us _________ this house.

    a. for   b. at   c. in   d. with

107. You must not press the matter _________ an unreasonable point as opinions are sharply divided _________ the question.

    a. between   b. on   c. to   d. in

108. Many farmers diverted water _________ the canal _________ their fields.

    a. with   b. in   c. into   d. from

109. He seemed to be _________ a strange mood when I found him having a dig _________ his best friends.

    a. at   b. in   c. to   d. over

110. These days his reputation is _________ a cloud as all his activities are shrouded _________ mystery.

    a. with   b. in   c. under   d. over

ANSWERS

1. b, d	**2.** a, c	**25.** a, c	**26.** b, a
3. b, c	**4.** d, c	**27.** b, c	**28.** c, a
5. b, a	**6.** c, a	**29.** c, a	**30.** a, b
7. c, b	**8.** a, b	**31.** c, b	**32.** a, c
9. a, c	**10.** a, c	**33.** b, a	**34.** c, b
11. b, c	**12.** a, c	**35.** b, d	**36.** a, b
13. c, a	**14.** b, a	**37.** c, b	**38.** d, c
15. d, c	**16.** a, c	**39.** a, c	**40.** b, d
17. a, c	**18.** b, c	**41.** c, b	**42.** a, b
19. a, b	**20.** b, c	**43.** b, a	**44.** c, a
21. c, b	**22.** a, d	**45.** d, b	**46.** a, b
23. a, b	**24.** d, c	**47.** b, c	**48.** b, a

49. a, b	**50.** b, c	**81.** a, d	**82.** b, d
51. b, a	**52.** a, c	**83.** c, a	**84.** b, c
53. b, d	**54.** a, b	**85.** c, a	**86.** a, c
55. c, a	**56.** b, c	**87.** a, c	**88.** c, a
57. a, b	**58.** c, a	**89.** c, d	**90.** d, c
59. c, d	**60.** a, d	**91.** d, c	**92.** a, b
61. a, b	**62.** d, c	**93.** b, a	**94.** d, a
63. a, c	**64.** c, b	**95.** a, c	**96.** b, c
65. a, c	**66.** c, b	**97.** c, b	**98.** b, d
67. b, d	**68.** a, c	**99.** d, c	**100.** b, a
69. c, b	**70.** a, b	**101.** b, c	**102.** c, b
71. d, a	**72.** a, b	**103.** b, c	**104.** c, b
73. c, a	**74.** a, b	**105.** a, c	**106.** a, c
75. b, c	**76.** a, c	**107.** c, b	**108.** d, c
77. b, d	**78.** a, b	**109.** b, a	**110.** c, b
79. a, c	**80.** c, b		

૭૪

22. TEST PAPERS—I

Write sentences to illustrate the difference in meaning between the following:

(A)

1.	Act on	Act up to
2.	Agree with	Agree to
3.	Angry with	Angry at
4.	Apply to	Apply against
5.	Attend to	Attend up/on
6.	Beat about	Beat with
7.	Bear with	Bear down
8.	Break in	Break into
9.	Call in	Call for
10.	Come of	Come to
11.	Deal in	Deal with
12.	Differ with	Differ from
13.	Do without	Do away with
14.	Die of	Die with
15.	Fall to	Fall off
16.	Fall out with	Fall upon
17.	Go with	Go without
18.	Get at	Get over
19.	Live at/in	Live on
20.	Look for	Look into
21.	Sail against the wind	Sail before/with the wind

22.	Take to	Take up
23.	Stand by	Stand on
24.	Take after	Take off
25.	Wait for	Wait on

(B)

1.	Above all	After all
2.	All in all	All over
3.	In spite of	In the teeth of
4.	At home in English	Good at English
5.	In general	In the best interest of
6.	Get rid of	Get the wind of
7.	In time	On time
8.	Of one's own accord	Of the view
9.	Of the same block	Of the first water
10.	At the hotel	In the hotel
11.	In the room	Into the room
12.	In the corner	On the corner

(C)

1.	Slow at	Slow of
2.	Blind of	Blind to
3.	Born at/in	Born of
4.	Delighted at	Delighted in
5.	Famous for	Famous with
6.	Quick of	Quick at
7.	Subject to	Subjected to

ANSWERS

(A)

1. He acted on my advice.
   We should act up to our convictions.

2. I do not agree with you in this matter.
   He agreed to my proposal.

3. Why are you angry with him?
   He was angry at your behaviour.

4. I have applied to the principal for the post of a teacher.
   She has applied against you to the officer.

5. Please attended to me.
   I attended up/on some guests last evening.

6. Do not beat about the bush.
   He beat the dog with a stick.

7. Please bear with us in this matter.
   Akbar bore down all opposition.

8. The syce is breaking in the horse.
   Some burglar broke into his house last night.

9. Please call in the doctor.
   This matter calls for urgent attention.

10. She came of age yesterday.
    After Bickering, they came to blows.

11. He deals in sugar.
    It is not quite easy to deal with bullies.

12. I differ with you in this matter.
    This toy differs from that.

13. We can't do without air.

    The robbers did away with the trader.

14. He died of fever.

    She died with overwork.

15. They fell to quarrelling.

    The leaves of trees fall off in autumn.

16. The two friends fell out with each other.

    Our soldiers fell upon the enemy.

17. We have to go with others in social matters.

    It goes without saying that he is an honest man.

18. The fox could not get at the grapes.

    At last I got over all obstacles.

19. He lives at Behrampura.

    I live in Delhi.

    The cow lives on grass.

20. What are you looking for here?

    Please look into this matter.

21. It is not so easy to sail against the wind.

    Anybody can sail before/with the wind.

22. She took her mother's death to heart.

    I shall take up the matter with him.

23. I'll always stand by you.

    Don't stand on ceremonies.

24. She takes after her mother.

    I took off my shoes before entering the temple.

25. I'm waiting for him.

    We had to wait on the minister for two hours.

(B)

1. He is, above all, a man of integrity.

After all, he is my friend.

2. He is all in all in this office.

Pollution has spread all over the world.

3. In spite of his opposition, I was able to get the proposal accepted.

The bill was carried out in the teeth of opposition.

4. He is at home in English.

She is good at English.

5. In general, this proposal is acceptable to all.

This scheme is in the best interest of common people.

6. It is not so easy to get rid of bad habits.

Somehow, he has got the wind of our plans.

7. I reached the station in time.

The train arrived at the station on time.

8. She went with her husband of her own accord.

I'm of the view that corruption should not be allowed to flourish at any cost.

9. They are chips of the same block.

He is a fool of the first water.

10. We'll meet at the hotel Regal.

There are many rooms in this hotel.

11. He is sitting in the room.

She came into the room.

12. A coin is lying in the corner of the room.

His shop is situated on the corner of the road.

(C)

1. She is slow at arithmetic.

   He is slow of hearing.

2. He is blind of one eye.

   She is blind to her son's faults.

3. He was born at Gobindgarh.

   I was born in Mumbai.

   He was born of rich parents.

4. I am greatly delighted at this news.

   He is delighted in visiting new lands.

5. Delhi is famous for the Red fort.

   Tagore is famous with Indians.

6. She is quick of learning.

   He is quick at solving sums in Mathematics.

7. This bill is subject to the approval of the President.

   The prisoners were subjected to untold modes of torture.

In the following passages, please point out the part of speech of each of the words which are italicised.

(1)

To Mr. and Mrs. Gardiner he was *scarcely* a less interesting personage than *to herself*. They had *long* wished to see him. The whole party *before* them, indeed, existed a *lively* attention. The *suspicions which* had just arisen of Mr. Darcy and their niece directed their observation *towards each* with an earnest, though guarded inquiry; and they soon drew from those inquiries the full conviction that one of them at least knew what it was to love. Of the lady's sensations they remained a little *in doubt*; but that the gentleman was overflowing *with* admiration was evident enough.

Elizabeth, *on* her side, had much to do. She wanted to ascertain the feelings of each of her visitors, she wanted to compose her own, and to make herself *agreeable* to all; *and* in the latter object, *where* she feared most to fail, she was most sure of success,.........

(2)

To put *that* (a) *into perspective* the next most successful active driver in terms of race victories is Briton David Coulthard *with* a mere 13 *over* a decade.

This year the champion can *overhaul* Ayrton Senna's landmark tally of 65 pole positions—Schumacher *needs* just two more to equal the late Brazilian's feat— and also move a big step closer to an *extraordinary* 100 wins.

There can be no doubt *that* (b) he would like that century, *even if* it looks to be a tall order *with* a Ferrari contract *due* to expire at the *end* of 2006.

(3)

"The date *of* execution of the death *sentence* fixed by the trial judge, if any, may be stayed till the *disposal* of the petition *already* received *by* the President of India *on behalf of* these prisoners," the Director (Judicial), Home, said in *his* communication.

The communication, a copy of which was made *available* to the *media* here today, said the prisoners might be *allowed* seven days' time *for* submitting mercy petitions to the President under Article 72 of the Constitution.

The *period* may be counted from the day of which they were *informed* of the Tamil Nadu Governor rejecting their petitions, it said.

Their mercy *petitions* may be forwarded to the Ministry of Home Affairs *along with* the state government's comments and relevant documents *without* delay, the communication *added.*

The date of execution was *originally* fixed for November 5 but it was *indefinitely* stayed by the jail authorities to enable the convicts to seek Presidential *reprieve.*

(4)

For increasing exports *substantially, and in* the process, trying to become *international,* managements should *consider* the possibility of entering *into* a *strategic* alliance with a company abroad. *This* could take *various* forms such as a licensing agreement, a joint venture or a research or marketing cooperation arrangements.

Some kind of an alliance is, *however, desirable,* as starting something fresh, *especially* in a *developed* country, is extremely difficult, and the cost of developing a customer base or dealer *network* is *often prohibitive.*

(5)

Others, however, were made to strengthen the powers of the police, *who feel increasingly* restricted *by* the *growing* number of regulations and guidelines imposed in *recent* years, and increasingly disrespected by the public. The Commission proposes, for example, to continue allowing confessions unaccompanied by other evidence as sufficient for a *guilty* verdict, *while* many human rights groups had been calling for an end to uncorroborated confessions. Liberty says: "Uncorroborated confession evidence *remains* one of the biggest *single* causes of innocent people going to prison."

(6)

We *have hard* work ahead. There is no *resting* for any one of us *till* we redeem our *pledge* in full, till we make all the people of India what *destiny intended* them to be. We are citizens of a great country, on the *verge of bold* advance, and we have to live up to that high standard. All of us, to whatever religion we may *belong*, are *equally* the children of India with equal rights, privileges and obligations. We cannot *encourage* communalism or narrow-mindedness, for no nation can be great whose people are *narrow* in thought or in action.

To the nations and peoples of the world we send greetings and *pledge* ourselves to co-operate with them *in* furthering peace, freedom and democracy.

And to India, our much-loved motherland, the ancient, the eternal and the ever-new, we pay our *reverent homage* and we *bind ourselves afresh* to *her* service.

— J.L. Nehru

(7)

The hume pipes laid *underneath* the *plant* to carry the storm water of the nullah have *burst* due to heavy rain as these proved *inadequate*. Consequently, *several* parts of the project have developed *wide* cracks and the main supporting masonary wall and the embankment *along* the nullah have also started caving in. The maturation yard has also started sinking and the garbage platform is facing *collapse. If* immediate *protective* measures are not taken, the *entire* project, along with machinery worth Rs. 1.5 crore, may be washed away.

The report further explains that—

Wrong site selection, *faulty* design and substandard construction work have been *mainly responsible* for the *virtual* collapse of the project.

(8)

Everybody is today talking about *human* rights, rights of women, rights of children, rights of refugees, rights of workers, rights of prisoners and so on.

One *important aspect* of this rights movement is the rights of farmers which are now more and more being highlighted, though *still* not *quite adequately according to* the *specific needs* of poor and *marginal* farmers. Still, all *positive* steps in this direction must be welcomed.

(9)

With better capacity *utilization,* these projects would be *able to plough* back profits for expansion and even *contribute* funds for the country's *general* development—a task that they should have started years *ago.* The failure in this regard can be partly ascribed to shortages of *raw* material. *Especially* steel and coal, and to the *frequent* disruptions in both power supply and rail transport. On *top* of it all, there are the crippling labour *tussles* and the frequent strikes for higher wages which hold up *productive* processes—with the *inevitable* chain reaction. On none of these fronts can the public sector *validly* claim *lasting* improvements. There are far too many sick giants *even now,* and the net *returns* on the total Central investment of Rs. 5.588 crores in this sector continue to be *utterly disproportionate.*

(10)

The electronic book is *here*. Gone are the days in which we had to carry along heavy tomes on trips. The *new* wonder item is called Rocket book and gets its *reading* material *directly from* the Internet. It *has room* for *about* ten novels, the texts of which appear crystal *clear on* the screen. It *weighs only* 600 gms and costs about Rs. 20,000. At present, only English language novels are *available* from the Internet. The price of the downloaded books will be *significantly* lower than printed texts.

ANSWERS

(1)

(i)	Scarcely	— adverb
(ii)	to	— preposition
(iii)	herself	— pronoun
(iv)	long	— adverb
(v)	before	— preposition
(vi)	lively	— adjective
(vii)	suspicions	— noun
(viii)	which	— relative pronoun (and conjunction)
(ix)	towards	— preposition
(x)	each	— pronoun
(xi)	in	— preposition
(xii)	doubt	— noun
(xiii)	with	— preposition
(xiv)	on	— preposition
(xv)	agreeable	— adjective
(xvi)	and	— conjunction
(xvii)	where	— relative adverb (and conjunction)

**(2)

(i)	that (a)	—	pronoun
(ii)	into	—	preposition
(iii)	perspective	—	noun
(iv)	with	—	preposition
(v)	over	—	preposition
(vi)	this	—	demonstrative) determiner (and pronoun)
(vii)	overhaul	—	verb
(viii)	needs	—	verb
(ix)	extraordinary	—	adjective
(x)	that (b)	—	conjunction
(xi)	even if	—	conjunction
(xii)	with	—	preposition
(xiii)	due	—	adjective
(xiv)	end	—	noun.

**(3)

(i)	The	—	determiner (article and demonstrative adjective)
(ii)	of	—	preposition
(iii)	sentence	—	noun
(iv)	disposal	—	noun
(v)	already	—	adverb
(vi)	by	—	preposition
(vii)	on behalf of	—	preposition
(viii)	his	—	(possessive) determiner (adjective and pronoun)
(ix)	available	—	adjective
(x)	media	—	noun
(xi)	allowed	—	preposition

(xii)	for	—	preposition
(xiii)	period	—	noun
(xiv)	informed	—	verb
(xv)	their	—	determiner
(xvi)	petitions	—	noun
(xvii)	along with	—	preposition
(xviii)	without	—	preposition
(xix)	added	—	verb
(xx)	originally	—	adverb
(xxi)	indefinitely	—	adverb
(xxii)	reprieve	—	noun

(4)

(i)	For	—	preposition
(ii)	substantially	—	adverb
(iii)	international	—	adjective
(iv)	consider	—	verb
(v)	into	—	preposition
(vi)	strategic	—	adjective
(vii)	this	—	pronoun
(viii)	various	—	adjective
(ix)	some	—	determiner
(x)	however	—	adverb
(xi)	desirable	—	adjective
(xii)	especially	—	adverb
(xiii)	developed	—	adjective
(xiv)	network	—	noun
(xv)	often	—	adverb
(xvi)	prohibitive	—	adjective

(5)

(i)	others	—	pronoun
(ii)	who	—	relative pronoun
(iii)	feel	—	verb
(iv)	increasingly	—	adverb
(v)	by	—	preposition
(vi)	growing	—	adjective
(vii)	recent	—	adjective
(viii)	guilty	—	adjective
(ix)	while	—	conjunction
(x)	remains	—	verb
(xi)	single	—	adjective.

(6)

(i)	have	—	verb
(ii)	hard	—	adjective
(iii)	resting	—	noun
(iv)	till	—	conjunction
(v)	pledge	—	noun
(vi)	destiny	—	noun
(vii)	intended	—	verb
(viii)	verge	—	noun
(ix)	of	—	preposition
(x)	bold	—	adjective
(xi)	belong	—	verb
(xii)	equally	—	adverb
(xiii)	encourage	—	verb
(xiv)	narrow	—	adjective
(xv)	in	—	preposition
(xvi)	reverent	—	adjective

(xvii)	homage	—	noun
(xviii)	bind	—	verb
(xix)	ourselves	—	pronoun
(xx)	afresh	—	adverb
(xxi)	her	—	determiner.

(7)

(i)	underneath	—	preposition
(ii)	plant	—	noun
(iii)	burst	—	verb
(iv)	inadequate	—	adjective
(v)	several	—	adjective
(vi)	wide	—	adjective
(vii)	along	—	preposition
(viii)	collapse	—	noun
(ix)	If	—	conjunction
(x)	protective	—	adjective
(xi)	entire	—	adjective
(xii)	faulty	—	adjective
(xiii)	mainly	—	adverb
(xiv)	responsible	—	adjective
(xv)	virtual	—	adjective

(8)

(i)	Everybody	—	pronoun
(ii)	human	—	adjective
(iii)	important	—	adjective
(iv)	aspect	—	noun
(v)	still	—	adverb
(vi)	quite	—	adverb
(vii)	adequately	—	adverb

(viii)	according to	—	preposition
(ix)	specific	—	adjective
(x)	needs	—	noun
(xi)	marginal	—	adjective
(xii)	positive	—	adjective

(9)

(i)	With	—	preposition
(ii)	utilization	—	noun
(iii)	able	—	adjective
(iv)	to plough	—	infinitive
(v)	contribute	—	verb
(vi)	general	—	adjective
(vii)	ago	—	adverb
(viii)	raw	—	adjective
(ix)	especially	—	adverb
(x)	frequent	—	adjective
(xi)	top	—	noun
(xii)	tussles	—	noun
(xiii)	productive	—	adjective
(xiv)	inevitable	—	adjective
(xv)	validly	—	adverb
(xvi)	lasting	—	adjective
(xvii)	returns	—	noun
(xviii)	utterly	—	adverb
(xix)	disproportionate	—	adjective
(xx)	even now	—	adverb

(10)

(i)	The	—	determiner (article)
(ii)	here	—	adverb

(iii)	new	—	adjective
(iv)	reading	—	adjective
(v)	directly	—	adverb
(vi)	from	—	preposition
(vii)	has	—	verb
(viii)	room	—	noun
(ix)	about	—	preposition
(x)	clear	—	adjective
(xi)	on	—	preposition
(xii)	weighs	—	verb
(xiii)	only	—	adverb
(xiv)	available	—	adjective
(xv)	significantly	—	adverb.

ॐ

24. TEST PAPERS—III

Please find out at least 5 prepositions in each of the following passages. Also point out the noun or pronoun each preposition governs. You are not to mention any preposition more than once—unless it governs a different noun or pronoun.

(1)

A large number of players and others were put several questions in the context of betting and match-fixing. Nobody said that it was good, insignificant or pardonable. Of course, at the initial stage, many did not believe that such a thing could happen. In fact, Cronje had such a good reputation that even the government of his own country could not believe the Delhi Police when a type-recorded dialogue between Cronje and a bookie, was released. Many said that perhaps it was fabricated or wrongly collected by the Delhi Police with intentions good or bad.

(2)

The Appointed Day has come—the day appointed by destiny—and India stands forth again after long slumber and struggle, awake, vital, free and independent . The past clings on to us still in some measure and we have to do much before we redeem the pledges we have so often taken. Yet the turning point is past, and history begins anew for us, the history which we shall live and act and others will write about.

It is a fateful moment for us in India, for all Asia and for the world. A new star rises, the star of freedom in the East, a new hope comes into being, a vision long cherished materializes. May the star never set and that hope never be betrayed!

We rejoice in that freedom, even though clouds surround us, and many of our people are sorrow stricken and difficult problems encompass us. But freedom brings responsibilities and burdens and we have to face them in the spirit of a free and disciplined people.

—J.L. Nehru

(3)

One bane of the stock market is the widespread undertaking of speculative transaction which, though legally allowed, subject to certain laws, rules and regulations, ruins many investors because either they overshoot themselves or violate the laws and rules deliberately for greediness and attempt at grabbing at quick and easy luck.

Sec. 45(5) defines "Speculative transaction means a transaction in which a contract for the purchase or sale of any commodity, including stock and shares, is periodically or ultimately settled otherwise than by the actual delivery or transfer of the commodity or scrips."

There is a proviso to the section 45(5) which adumbrates certain exceptions in which cases a transaction shall not be deemed to be a speculative one:

(a) a contract in respect of raw material or....

(b) a contract in respect of stocks and shares entered into by a dealer or investor therein to guard against loss in his holdings of stocks and shares through price fluctuation.

(c) a contract entered into by a member of a forward market or a stock exchange in the course of any transaction in the nature of jobbing or arbitrage to guard against loss which may arise in the ordinary course of his business as such member."

(4)

Since roughly the past three hundred years, the world had changed more than it may have done in the preceding thousand. Science, technology, capital enterprise, adventurism and initiative contributed to immense generation of wealth and military power as a result of which small sections of the world raced ahead, propelled by these early advantages. Sadly, as new and progressive concepts for the creation and management of human resources were developed by the states that claimed to be leaders of the world, these states completely ignored the basic elements of human existence, that is, the value of human life.

(5)

It was noticed that whenever the boy had a quarrel or an argument with his parents he had a sense of injustice as he felt that they favoured his younger brother. It was then that he would see this dream. He would, in his anger, link their act of injustice with the ugliness of a crow. It was an association he had made in innocence in his childhood which had endured into adulthood, but with time he had forgotten why he had formed the association.

(6)

Mars is a planet of force and energy. It is gratifying to note that it is in a benevolent mood and promises make this a perfect time for you. Pleasure, romance, love and laughter, will come your way. It may take some time, but there is a strong indication of an improvement in all personal affairs.

(7)

The industrial countries are confronted by an increasing volume of residual waste. In France alone, flyash form the incineration of household waste amounts to about 30000 tons per annum. There is clearly no possibility of releasing these materials, rich in heavy metals, untreated into the environment.

The aim of stabilization processes is to prevent potentially toxic components such as heavy metals or chlorinated compounds from being carried away by rainwater or surface waters.

The stabilization techniques, involving beaching-edge expertise in chemistry, mechanical engineering and thermal engineering, operate through the addition of mineral or hydraulic binders or the addition of organic binders to residual waste.

(8)

It weighs half a kilogram and can be operated by tensing two muscles in the user's forearm where two electrodes—one for each muscle—read the tiny electrical signals, which are amplified and fed into a series of circuits, prompting the fingers to curl up. The hand can pick things up between two or three fingers to clasp an object in a fist.

(9)

"Writing is therapeutic and there is a lot of truth in the lines that every writer sheds his sickness in his writings. Believe me if I hadn't gone through some very trying periods in life—a divorce, a 15-year-long litigation battle, monetary stress, failed relationships, then I couldn't have written so much, for each setback was countered by writing, more and more..... "

And on his looking much less than his actual years, he lets out a moral: "Empty your mind for some time and let it wander aimlessly and then walk for at least one hour a day it keeps away all possible diseases."

(10)

Moon surrounded by malefic stars becomes a serious liability. You might feel betrayed even by those close to you. If you insist on trying to help people, you are likely to be misunderstood. There will be very little understanding with the people around. The best course is not to react to the ugly situations you are expected to experience during this time.

A hasty decision needs to be guarded against during the first quarter. You will feel ignored by a loved one during the second.

A tiring journey should be on the anvil during the third, you could, however, sort out a pending task during the end part.

(11)

The new year starts on a good note. No doubts, it is a comparatively busier year but you will be able to shoulder your responsibilities quite easily. The starry position reveals you will examine each and every option with deep thought and insight. You should not, however, expect a thumping success in the beginning but you are not going to lag behind when the year advances further. If you are a student especially of arts group, you will show reasonably good progress in your studies. If working, you can expect things to go your way.

(12)

Moreover, what is required is not such material advancement as would make us slaves of what we created with our hands, but an all round awakening and the realization of the supreme goal of life.

In fact, man has developed his intellect at the expense of spirituality. The tendency cannot be better described than in the words of H.G. Wells, who says that "the future man will be bold, teethless and devoid of emotions."

The supreme things in life have to be realized and understood in their totality. Since our mind can only analyse, the highest stages in life are beyond its reach. Science is not enough to know the truth and some other human faculty must be there to probe into the realities of nature. The expansiveness of outlook is a matter that can be accomplished only by the integration of science and spirituality.

(13)

The security cover of the seven-nation conglomerate was enough to keep the bad guys off the games.

Many were surprised at the way the Athenians obeyed the special traffic rules, including leaving Olympic lanes for the

Olympic family for a month. There were no traffic jams and no snarls.

A week before the games started, hotel workers and others went on strike, demanding better wages. But the games were free of labour problems and strikes.

Greece was one of the economically weaker nations to host the games. Many had thought that increased power demand would lead to blackouts and power cuts in the Olympic village. But the fears were unfounded.

(14)

If in a democracy the nation can be held to ransom by strikes in public utility services hell with it. Such strikes are primarily politically motivated and should be ruthlessly put down. In a country, where a great majority of people live under or on the border line of hunger, strikes by well-paid railwaymen drawing salaries many times the average national income and always clamouring for more and more are most ignoble. Have they no consideration for the common man who is made to suffer as if the present economic conditions are not enough to worry him? It is time the railwaymen retraced their steps so as to avoid the wrath of the public at large.

Strikes, as a rule, should be banned in essential services. People employed therein may have genuine demands and grievances, which should forthwith be referred to a high-powered commission, presided over by an eminent retired judge of the Supreme Court, for expeditious and final adjudication. This would put an end to strikes in such vital services. Trade Union activities should normally reserved for private sector enterprises when they are rapacious and the workers do not get a fair deal.

(15)

To India, rapid expansion of resources, coupled with sizable employment opportunities would be compensation enough. Besides, such facilities have been confined to sectors which could return the credits from exports to Iran. The prices payable for Indian material remain unspecified, but there is no reason to believe that Iran will prove as tough a bargainer as the Soviet Union and Japan. The proposed joint shipping line would be the first venture of its kind. With Iran's sound financial backing, it is likely to prove beneficial to the entire region. All told, the economic partnership now forged may prove to be the precursor of friendlier ties in other spheres. It promises to make the two decades old tensions a bad dream.

(16)

The two day emergency meeting of the International Cricket Council was held at the Lord's, London. One of the proposals was that the number of one-day games be slashed in the wake of the match-fixing and betting.

One of the proposals to be considered was that Cronje as well as three English players alleged by the former all-rounder Chris Levis to have been in the payroll of bookies and cricketers worldwide be offered "amnesty" for providing information to the authorities about corruption in the game.

(17)

Evidently, pressures from several sides and State Ministers' endless recommendations have led to heavy recruitment of staff at all levels in the public sector. Parkinson's principle has been in operation with a vengeance. An immediate problem, therefore, is to find work for employees who are contributing little to the output.

(18)

What contribution such advertisements made to turning the non-railway public against the strikers remains to be determined. So far as the Government was concerned, its approach left no room for doubt. The Government was resolved not to be pushed around by railway workers or to wear velvet gloves in handling them. In Britain and the USA, where the militant trade unions have far more money to spend, there would probably have been a counter-campaign by the strikers, and the newspapers in those countries would have published it too. By and large, however, the striking railwaymen in our country did not seem to have too good a case. This was further damaged by incidents of sabotage.

According to some of the Prime Minister's colleagues, the Government's minimum likely gain from its firm handling of the situation is a strong discouragement to prospective strikers in State undertakings which maintain some of the vital public services in the country. Public opinion is seen as a variable feature of Indian life, and success is viewed as an irresistible magnet for public support. The truth is that our people are sick and tired of disruption, and even if they do not themselves help to restore sanity. They are with the Establishment when the latter shows genuine signs of purposeful action.

(19)

A huge reserve of natural gas capable of generating 2680 MW of power annually for 30 years has been detected in Rajasthan's border district of Barmer.

Seven block areas of Barmer have been found to possess coal-based methane reserve which could be gainfully exploited for the state's economic development, according to an official report made available here.

An estimated 30 per cent of the hidden natural resource could be made use of, it said.

The report projected that an estimated investment of about Rs. 6300 crore to tap the reserve could fetch the state an annual revenue of Rs. 492 crore by way of 10 per cent royalty and another 12 per cent sales tax.

Besides its use in different forms, the exploitation of the gas could produce water for irrigation and domestic consumption after proper treatment.

The findings were based on detailed investigations carried out by different agencies during the past 16 years.

The report also spoke of existence of extensive lignite deposits in various parts in the western region of the state, mostly in the desert areas. Seismic surveys carried out during 1996 indicated extensive presence of thick lignite seams in Barmer graben, which is now considered as the "northern continuity of the Cambay basin."

The coal-based methane had been detected in commercial quantities in the sub-surface lignite deposits of the Cambay basin, which had raised hopes for possible exploitation for bettering the state's economic health. The report also indicated the presence of similar gas in the Sanchore well number one, drilled by the Oil and Natural Gas Corporation.

The coal beds located in the region could be exploited commercially with standard production techniques, the report said.

ANSWERS

Preposition	Noun/pronoun governed by each preposition
	(1)
(i) of	players
(ii) in	context
(iii) of	betting
(iv) at	stage
(v) of	country
(vi) between	Cronje, bookie
(vii) by	police
(viii) with	intentions
	(2)
(i) by	destiny
(ii) after	slumber

Preposition		Noun/pronoun governed by prepositions
(iii)	to	us
(iv)	in	measure
(v)	for	us
(vi)	about	history
(vii)	for	Asia
(viii)	for	world
(ix)	of	freedom
(x)	in	East
(xi)	into	being
(xii)	of	people
(xiii)	in	spirit

(3)

Preposition		Noun/pronoun governed by prepositions
(i)	of	stock market
(ii)	of	transactions
(iii)	to	laws, rules, regulations
(iv)	for	greediness
(v)	at	grabbing
(vi)	at	buck
(vii)	in	which
(viii)	for	purchase, sale
(ix)	of	commodity, stocks, shares
(x)	by	delivery, transfer
(xi)	of	commodity, scrips
(xii)	to	section 45(5)
(xiii)	in respect of	stocks, shares
(xiv)	into	contract
(xv)	by	dealer, investor

Preposition		**Noun/pronoun governed by prepositions**
(xvi)	against	loss
(xvii)	in	holdings
(xviii)	through	(price) fluctuation
(xix)	by	member
(xx)	of	transaction
(xxi)	in	nature
(xxii)	of	jobbing, arbitrage
(xxiii)	in	course
(xxiv)	of	(his) business

(4)

(i)	since	years
(ii)	in	thousand (years)
(iii)	to	generation
(iv)	of	wealth, power
(v)	of	which
(vi)	of	world
(vii)	by	advantages
(viii)	for	creation, management
(ix)	of	resources
(x)	by	states
(xi)	of	existence
(xii)	of	life

(5)

(i)	with	(his) parents
(ii)	of	injustice
(iii)	in	anger
(iv)	of	crow

Preposition		**Noun/pronoun governed by prepositions**
(v)	in	innocence
(vi)	in	childhood
(vii)	into	adulthood
(viii)	with	time

(6)

(i)	of	force, energy
(ii)	in	mood
(iii)	for	you
(iv)	of	improvement
(v)	in	affairs

(7)

(i)	by	volume
(ii)	of	waste
(iii)	In	France
(iv)	from	incineration
(v)	to, about	tons
(vi)	per	annum
(vii)	of	releasing
(viii)	into	environment
(ix)	of	(stabilization) processes
(x)	from	being carried (away)
(xi)	by	rainwater, (surface) waters,
(xii)	in	chemistry,(mechanical engineering), (thermal engineering)
(xiii)	through	addition
(xiv)	of	binders, addition
(xv)	to	waste

Preposition	Noun/pronoun governed by prepositions
	(8)
(i) by	tensing
(ii) in	(user's) forearm
(iii) for	muscle
(iv) into	series
(v) of	circuits
(vi) between	fingers
(vii) in	fist
	(9)
(i) of	truth
(ii) in	lines
(iii) in	writings
(iv) through	periods
(v) in	life
(vi) for	setback
(vii) by	writing
(viii) on	looking
(ix) than	years
(x) for	time
(xi) for	hour
	(10)
(i) by	stars
(ii) by	those
(iii) to	you
(iv) on	trying
(v) with	people
(vi) to	situations

Preposition		**Noun/pronoun governed by prepositions**
(vii)	during	time
(viii)	against	decision
(ix)	during	quarter
(x)	by	one
(xi)	during	second (quarter)
(xii)	on	anvil
(xiii)	during	third (quarter)
(xiv)	during	(end) part

(11)

(i)	on	note
(ii)	with	thought, insight
(iii)	in	beginning
(iv)	in	studies
(v)	of	(arts) group

(12)

(i)	of	what
(ii)	with	hands
(iii)	of	goal
(iv)	of	life
(v)	In	fact
(vi)	at	expense
(vii)	of	spirituality
(viii)	in	words
(ix)	of	H.G.Wells
(x)	of	emotions
(xi)	in	life
(xii)	in	totality

Preposition	Noun/pronoun governed by prepositions
(xiii) beyond	reach
(xiv) into	realities
(xv) of	nature
(xvi) of	outlook
xvii) by	integration
(xviii) of	science, spirituality

(13)

Preposition	Noun/pronoun governed by prepositions
(i) of	(seven-nation) conglomerate
(ii) off	games
(iii) at	way
(iv) for	(Olympic) family
(v) for	month
(vi) before	games
(vii) on	strike
(viii) of	problems, strikes
(ix) of	nations
(x) to	blackouts, power cuts
(xi) in	(Olympic) village

(14)

Preposition	Noun/pronoun governed by prepositions
(i) in	democracy
(ii) to	ransom
(iii) by	strike
(iv) in	(public utility) services
(v) with	it
(vi) In	country
(vii) of	people
(viii) under, on	(border) line

Preposition		Noun/pronoun governed by prepositions
(ix)	of	hunger
(x)	by	railwaymen
(xi)	for	more and more (income)
(xii)	for	(common) man
(xiii)	of	public
(xiv)	at	large
(xv)	in	(essential) services
(xvi)	to	commission
(xvii)	over	commission
(xviii)	by	judge
(xix)	of	Supreme Court
(xx)	for	adjudication
(xxi)	to	strikes
(xxii)	in	(vital) services
(xxiii)	for	(private sector) enterprises

(15)

(i)	To	India
(ii)	of	resources
(iii)	with	opportunites
(iv)	to	sectors
(v)	from	exports
(vi)	to	Iran
(vii)	for	(Indian) material
(viii)	of	(its) kind
(ix)	with	backing
(x)	to	region
(xi)	of	ties
(xii)	in	spheres

Preposition	Noun/pronoun governed by prepositions
	(16)
(i) of	International Cricket Council
(ii) at	(the) Lord's
(iii) of	proposals
(iv) of	(one-day) games
(v) in the wake of	match-fixing, betting
(vi) by	(all-rounder) Chris Lewis
(vii) in	payroll
(viii) of	bookies, cricketers
(ix) for	providing
(x) to	authorities
(xi) about	corruption
(xii) in	game
	(17)
(i) from	sides
(ii) to	recruitment
(iii) of	staff
(iv) at	levels
(v) in	(public) sector
(vi) in	operation
(vii) with	(a) vengeance
(viii) to	output
	(18)
(i) to	turning
(ii) against	strikes
(iii) for	doubt

Preposition		**Noun/pronoun governed by prepositions**
(iv)	by	(railway) workers
(v)	in	handling
(vi)	In	Britain, USA
(vii)	by	strikers
(viii)	in	countries
(ix)	in	country
(x)	by	incidents
(xi)	of	sabotage
(xii)	According to	some
(xiii)	from	handling
(xiv)	of	situation
(xv)	to	strikers
(xvi)	in	(state) undertakings
(xvii)	of	(public) services
(xviii)	of	(Indian) life
(xix)	for	(public) support
(xx)	of	disruption
(xxi)	with	Establishment
(xxii)	of	action

(19)

(i)	of	gas
(ii)	of	generating
(iii)	of	power
(iv)	for	(30) years
(v)	in	(border) district
(vi)	of	Barmer
(vii)	for	development

Preposition		**Noun/pronoun governed by prepositions**
(viii)	according to	report
(ix)	per	cent
(x)	in	forms
(xi)	for	irrigation, consumption
(xii)	after	treatment
(xiii)	on	investigations
(xiv)	by	agencies
(xv)	during	(16) years
(xvi)	of	existence
(xvii)	of	deposits
(xviii)	in	parts
(xix)	in	region
(xx)	of	state
(xxi)	in	areas
(xxii)	during	1996
(xxiii)	of	seams
(xxiv)	in	(Barmer) graben
(xxv)	of	(Cambay) basin
(xxvi)	in	quantities
(xxvii)	for	exploitation
(xxviii)	for	bettering
(xxix)	by	Oil and Natural Gas Commission
(xxx)	with	(production) techniques

ೞ ೲ

| Your Space |

Your Space